THE HOUSE & GARDEN BOOK OF
COUNTRY GARDENS

THE HOUSE & GARDEN BOOK OF
COUNTRY GARDENS

CHARLES QUEST-RITSON

Condé Nast Books
London Sydney Auckland Johannesburg

For Brigid and the children, as ever

First published in 1998 by Condé Nast Books,
an imprint of Random House UK Ltd
20 Vauxhall Bridge Road, London SW1V 2SA

Random House Australia (Pty) Ltd
20 Alfred Street, Milsons Point, Sydney,
New South Wales 2061 Australia

Random House New Zealand
18 Poland Road, Glenfield, Auckland 10,
New Zealand

Random House South Africa (Pty) Ltd
Endulini, 5a Jublilee Road, Parktown 2193,
South Africa

Random House UK Limited Reg. No. 954009

Designed by Alison Shackleton
Edited by Emma Callery

A catalogue record for this book is available
from the British Library

ISBN 0 09 186372 42

Colour reproduction by Colorlito Rigogliosi s.r.l., Milan
Printed and bound in Singapore by Tien Wah Press

Contents

Introduction

By what criteria do we select the gardens that end up between the covers of *House & Garden*? Well, as Charles Quest-Ritson says in his article on Helen Dillon's Dublin garden, 'the best modern gardens combine strong formal design with interesting plants and good plantings'. That is certainly part of the story. But these need matching with individual expressions and a generous dollop of romance. The gardens in the book, all featured in the last decade of *House & Garden*, are owned or managed by people who love their gardens almost to the point of obsession. The colourist plantings at Sticky Wicket are in a constant state of fine-tuning, Shirley Cargill of Elsing Hall would probably find it as hard to say no to a rose as a dog lover would a stray, and anyone, like me, who has spied Arabella Lennox-Boyd emerge from a plant sale has witnessed joyous fanaticism at work!

But despite all the feverish creativity and labour behind the making of these gardens, they all become places of great contentment to the owners, and inspiration to those who visit them. Remember that what you are seeing here is but a fleeting moment in each garden's year. Dixter is not all daffodils and spring bulbs, but an Aladdin's cave of innovative planting from one season to the next and the late Robin Spencer's garden at York Gate is as much a horticultural feast as a feat of engineering and imagination. Imagination is what you should find here in abundance and details to crib, like John Stefanidis' ingenious buns of *Hebe rakaiensis* under his fruit trees, Jim Reynolds' Gothicized bridge, looking like a palanquin floating over the Butterstream, and Jill Cowley's use of 'borrowed landscape' beyond her garden at Park Farm.

Devotees of Charles Quest-Ritson's succinct writing that made his book *The England Garden Abroad* such a success will find him true to form here, and despite having now seen these photographs more times that I can count, it is a tribute to the photographers that they seem as fresh and exciting as ever.

Tania Compton
Gardening Editor
House & Garden

WELL-STRUCTURED GARDENS

Bledlow Manor

When Lord and Lady Carrington came to Bledlow Manor some fifty years ago, there was barely a garden in existence. But in 1969 they engaged the young landscape architect Robert Adams, and now there are three distinct gardens to be enjoyed – the formal designs in front of the house, the Sculpture Garden across the back drive, and the Water Garden opposite. The development of each area has been a true partnership between the Carringtons and Robert Adams: every extension or alteration a joint decision.

Despite the limitations imposed by the garden's closeness to the village church and the Manor Farm, and the thin chalk soil, Robert Adams' eye for line and the use of space are the dominant features. Each area around the house is enclosed by hedges of beech, hornbeam or yew and great play is made throughout the garden of contrasts of

PREVIOUS PAGE The Armillary Garden with its iron sphere sitting at the centre surrounded by clipped hedges.

OPPOSITE The entrance to the Sculpture Garden is through a formal box-hedged garden cleverly designed so that there is a choice of four exits

BELOW St Peter presides over the bold formal beds in his garden. The brick path leads through to the next compartment, the Armillary Garden.

ABOVE Another fine element in this well-structured garden: the central path of the Walled Garden. The view here is of it leading past formally trained apple trees to a gazebo.

scale. Some of the compartments are small, whereas others really are very spacious. One of the smallest of the areas near to the house is St Peter's Garden, which is a quarter segment with a statue of St Peter from the palace of Westminster standing on a roughly hewn plinth at the apex. Box beds radiate out from the statue and for maximum effect, each division has been filled only with a single type of plant, including lavender, santolina, *Festuca glauca* and *Iris pallida* ssp. *pallida* 'Variegata'. Such bold planting in large groups is characteristic of every part of Bledlow Manor's garden.

St Peter's Garden is entered along a red brick path from the Pastel Garden, which in turn leads naturally into the Armillary Garden. The interplay between the materials – the ways in which they change between compartments or lead on into the next – is one of the best features of the design of the garden. Next comes the Armillary Garden, a formal topiary garden. In the centre is an elegant stone column with an iron sphere that reflects the surrounding great globes of yew resting on expertly maintained yew stands. The rest of the garden is then filled with smaller hedges of box designed to a regular geometric pattern; and these are complemented by the brick and different gravels of the paths and beds.

On the southern side of the house there is a walled courtyard with an avenue of *Viburnum carlesii* running down its centre to the Sunken Pool Garden at the end. The progression of the viburnums and the changes of levels in this area create a great sense of space. Inspired by an early visit to Hidcote, the Carringtons have also built a white-boarded pavilion above the pool in the Buckinghamshire vernacular.

As the Walled Garden is entered, there is a fine herbaceous border straight ahead of paeonies and delphiniums, backed by a hedge of hornbeam and beech. Then, in the middle of this walled area, is an octagonal gazebo whose trellised posts are planted with clematis and rambling roses. The central grass walk is lined with apple trees trained most architecturally as spheres around a wire globe: they rise from boxes of teucrium, each planted with a different herb such as sage, chives and Greek oregano. A recent addition to this garden is a mural of Vertumnus, the god of vegetation, depicted by Owen Turville in the Arcimboldi style as fruit and vegetables.

ABOVE TOP A bronze heron in the Sunken Pool Garden stands in a tangle of frozen cobwebs.

ABOVE Looking back from the central gazebo in the Walled Garden, the avenue of Viburnum carlesii *is an elegant walkway that leads the eye towards the pond.*

Across the back drive, behind Bledlow Manor, is the already remarkably mature 1-hectare (½-acre) Sculpture Garden – known as Church Close – started in 1991. Four paths radiate from the entrance gate as a four-pointed *patte-d'oie*. The garden has then been contoured to maximize the movement of the surface, and to give contrast between heights and depths. Its fluid design is a great foil to the more formal gardens near the house. A broad grass ride leads around a circuit and the sculptures occupy bays off it. They are screened by bold plantings of chunky shrubs so that only one piece of sculpture can be seen at a time. The presiding spirit is a splendid gorilla by Michael Cooper: it occupies a brick plinth backed by yews. Among other fine pieces are a cut pomegranate, pumpkins and gourds by Peter Randall Page.

Quite different in style, the 1.5-hectare (⅔-acre) Water Garden, was started in 1979 on the site of three old watercress beds. The thirteen springs which issue from its sides are the headwaters of the River Lyde, a tributary of the Thames. Water even runs from underneath the foundations of the church high up to the west. The steep valley sides have been so lushly planted with shrubs and herbaceous plants that at first the views are small and enclosed: the dense vegetation comes right to the edge of the path. At the bottom, however, a wooden walkway raised above the muddy sides meanders around the edge of the lakes, surrounded by candelabra primroses, hostas and astilbes nestling among somewhat larger-scale gunneras. Here, as in every part of the garden, strong, structural, sweeps of plants are combined with the firm unifying hand of a single architect working with imaginative owners.

ABOVE The informal lines of the Sculpture Garden provides the perfect setting for many lovely pieces, including Peter Randall Page's pomegranate, pumpkins and gourds.

ABOVE *A wooden walkway in the Japanese style leads around the lake at the foot of the Lyde Garden, the formal name for the Water Garden.*

LEFT *Clipped box cones provide a striking foreground for this ghostly glimpse across the Lyde Garden.*

Cock Crow Farm

John Stefanidis's garden in Dorset is one of the most exciting to be made in the last twenty years; all the more surprising then, that it is known only to the *cognoscenti*. The garden offers ingenious design and incorporates many rare plants in effective combinations that remain entirely in harmony with the landscape.

The approach passes through farm buildings, a disused cowstall, and a darkened loggia, and then the formal garden suddenly opens up in front. John Stefanidis has mastered the problems of designing and planting a living garden as skilfully as he designs and furnishes a living interior. The formal garden fills a large gravelled quadrangle, an open-air hall with ultra-modern box parterres at one end and a grid of apple trees rising from clouds of *Hebe rakaiensis* at the other. The effect is stunning, with shadows and symmetry, pattern and repetition working together to achieve a striking whole. All four sides of the formal garden are enclosed by the converted barns and cowstalls, some of brick and others wood-clad, which are now John Stefanidis's house.

Flints are often used throughout the garden, not only for paths but also as ornaments. A single 3-m (9-ft) pillar of flint in the courtyard breaks up the perfect symmetries of the area's design.

ABOVE Hostas, agapanthus and a clipped box cone stand in serried ranks in magnificent terracotta pots outside the covered loggia at the end of the courtyard.

RIGHT The lines of the modern parterre in the enclosed courtyard garden echo the long, low roofs of the house and outbuildings that surround the area.

Likewise, John Stefanidis's pugs, Bundi and Dainty, Hades and Bumpkin, are commemorated by a Brahmin bowl, filled with flints and placed on a plinth in the woodland garden and faced with yet more flints.

A small, formal herb garden runs off one end of the courtyard and an arch of *Viburnum carlesii* leads to the garden surrounding the house. There could be no greater contrast between the formal, enclosed and introspective world of the great courtyard and the expansive view of woodlands, wheat fields and downland which opens out as soon as you walk across the grass. The ground rises very gently away from the house to conceal a modern ha-ha, which brings the fields and meadows right to the edge of the lawn.

A broad specimen of *Pterocarya fraxinifolia*, planted in 1978, already fills its allotted space at the end of the lawn. The path behind it leads through thick plantings of the unusual *Eleagnus parvifolia* and into the 1-hectare (½ -acre) woodland garden, a miracle of good design and planting where a huge number of plants have been shoe-horned into a small area without any sense of overcrowding. A circle of limes is the central starting point for exploring the woodland. They have been clipped, interwoven and espaliered to form a circular frieze whose shadows play upon the grassy glade below. Six paths splay out from the lime circle. Some terminate in a firm feature, such as a dovecote or a pyramid of yew; others disappear under arches or curve out of sight. The confusion of choices – the sense that you want to

ABOVE A mighty flint-and-brick pillar to one side of the parterre creates an off-centre focal point. The flints were found in the ground when the garden was initially being created.

OPPOSITE Formally planted in rows and rigorously pruned, the apple trees in this orchard issue from great evergreen clumps of Hebe rakaiensis.

ABOVE The pebbled courtyard of a water garden. The surrounding plants – the hostas, euphorbias and Viburnum davidii – have been chosen for their architectural shapes.

OPPOSITE A paradox: this seat in the woodland garden has a fine view of the landscape as it is approached, but not when it is sat upon.

explore in every direction at once – is one of the great achievements of John Stefanidis's design in this part of his garden.

In one direction, a wisteria avenue leads to a secret rose garden, entirely enclosed by hornbeam hedges. Great rustic towers of wood enable the roses to scramble up, and fill the area with beauty and scent. Here is 'Robert Leopold', the seldom-seen apricot-coloured moss rose; the *wichurana* climber 'Weetwood' grows in the same tower as the Bourbon 'Blairii No 2'. Back at the lime circle and off in another direction, an inviting tunnel of hornbeam leads to a grove of the white-barked birch *Betula utilis,* underplanted with lamium and bluebells. A path doubles back through a grove of 20-m (65-ft) gum trees *Eucalyptus gunnii,* planted in 1980, to a glade where cyclamen have naturalized over a large area. Here, as everywhere, however, the plants are elements of design and decoration, parts of a greater scheme.

The circle of limes is backed by drifts of mahonias – mainly the hybrid called 'Charity' – but, throughout the woodland, evergreens

dominate: clipped domes of holly and Portugal laurel are interspersed with plants of *Skimmia japonica* and yew. The garden is very much in harmony with the wider landscape. The hollies, field maples and hazels of the hedgerows have been incorporated into the woodland garden: wild snowdrops and bluebells are part of the natural underplanting.

The garden is full of contrasts between little secret gardens and sudden extensive views. An enclosed garden fills a gap between two converted barns – no wider than the original entrance to the farmyard – but its yew boundary hedge is scalloped low to reveal a magnificent view north over the downs towards Blandford. In the woodland garden, there is a quiet, enclosed seat flanked by statues of a boy and a girl: but look over the hedge, and field after field stretch beyond. A circular pool edged with flint is entirely enclosed by a yew hedge. Next to it, however, a bamboo grove leads to a gate at the edge of the garden with another vast view of the Dorset landscape beyond. Surely was no garden so inventive, so satisfying and yet so much part of its countryside.

OPPOSITE The magnificent white Wisteria multijuga intermingles with a pale blue species on a Japanese-style pergola, which leads to a hidden rose-garden in the wood.

BELOW A small secret pool surrounded by a high yew hedge: the huge leaves of Gunnera manicata create a great contrast of scale.

ABOVE The tall posts and vivid blue paint of this gateway turn a decorative detail into a distinct element of design.

Hatfield House

When the present Marquess of Salisbury and his wife moved to Hatfield in 1972, Lady Salisbury had a major task on her hands reconstructing the garden in a style that is appropriate to this important historic house. She has been so successful that it is difficult to comprehend that much of what can be seen today is barely twenty-five years old. Hatfield's is probably the most ambitious – and certainly the most accomplished – neo-Jacobean garden ever to be made.

Lady Salisbury inherited some good features from earlier generations of Cecils. A square cloister of limes, trained into a pergola about 2.3m (7ft 6in) high, surrounds the gardens on the western side. It probably dates from the early 18th century and it encloses the yew-hedged Privy Garden, whose parterres were last laid out in the early 1900s by Lady Gwendoline Cecil, the unmarried daughter of Queen Victoria's prime minister, the 3rd Marquess. And on one of the lower terraces on the western side of the house lies the famous yew maze, laid out in 1840: by 1972, it was in desperate need of repair.

Lady Salisbury kept what was good, and replaced the meretricious. The Privy Garden was Lady Gwendoline's essay in neo-renaissance garden design, and very charming too. Lady Salisbury simply modernized the planting and gave more character to the outlines, so out came the hybrid teas and in went the David Austin English roses. The yews at the entrances were allowed to grow into elegantly tiered topiaries, and classical seats were tucked into the round corner bastions of yew.

ABOVE The immaculately clipped ilex avenues that run down either side of the East Garden.

OPPOSITE The evergreen outlines of the formal East Garden are much more substantial than the deciduous parkland beyond.

Lady Salisbury's first entirely new venture, then, was the Scented Garden, enclosed on three sides by ancient walls and by a clipped holly hedge on the fourth. The design is simple, based upon straight lines and circles, and every bed is filled with sweet-scented flowers. Part of it is laid out as a herb garden, reminiscent of the 17th-century interest in physick plants and pharmacology. The whole is a modern tribute to the sensory pleasures of gardens, and a link to the time when John Tradescant the Elder was head gardener at Hatfield.

The most impressive alterations made at Hatfield are to the formal East Garden, a private garden to which members of the public are allowed access one afternoon a week. It was laid out by Lord Salisbury's father as four square sections, each composed of four box-edged beds. Columns of yew march down the central avenue: the brick balustrading at the end is Victorian. In 1977, the present Lady Salisbury enclosed the garden on either side with avenues of evergreen oaks grown on 2-m (6ft 6in) stems and clipped like lollipops. She also added ornamental rugs of coloured cobbles in a simple star-shaped pattern at significant points around the outside.

BELOW A double staircase in the Renaissance style leads down from the house to the East Garden. Box-hedged beds are filled with clipped yew, old roses and shrubs to give bulk, and herbaceous groundwork for additional colour.

Each bed in the East Garden has a box topiary in the middle which divides it into four sections, producing four half-moons in each of the 16 beds, to be planted two-dimensionally rather than three. The plantings are mixed: old roses and shrubs give bulk, but the groundwork is herbaceous. The plantings are also completely random. There is some grading for height, but not for colour, though most of the flowers throughout the garden are chosen for their soft pastel shades. It is the formal design that holds the garden together.

The Knot Garden, begun in 1979 in front of the old palace, is the most successful historical

recreation at Hatfield House. It is built in the centre of the quad which was originally the courtyard of the palace, only one of whose sides remains. The designs are influenced by traditional English patterns from such herbaries as Parkinson's. Four central beds surround a small pool and the bed corners are marked by pyramids of box. Three are knots; the fourth is a gravel maze, to serve as a reminder that Hatfield might have had a maze when Queen Elizabeth I lived in the palace as a girl. The Elizabethan fruit garden is represented by pomegranates, put out in the summer, another link to the earliest gardens at Hatfield.

The Knot Garden is intended to be seen from the high walk around the perimeter, from which the Renaissance geometry can be best appreciated. The planting is true to the period too: every plant is one that would have been introduced to England before 1620. They include clove carnations, ancient roses, and a collection of historical tulips and narcissus given to Lady Salisbury by the Hortus Bulborum in Holland.

ABOVE A light dusting of snow throws the outlines of the authentically recreated Elizabethan Knot Garden into sharp relief.

OVERLEAF The spacious parterres of the East Garden look down towards the maze, lovingly restored since it was first created in the 19th century.

Work continues. The latest is a rehabilitation of the formal gardens on the southern side of the house, a private area that is rarely open to visitors. Here, two sunken gardens have been dug out, each with a fountain in the middle and surrounded by a raised walkway. Their beds are cut from the turf in patterns of stylized clover leaves, roses, oak leaves and fleur-de-lys, and the evergreen plantings will eventually form solid shapes in varying greens clipped at different heights.

Some years ago, Lady Salisbury wrote: 'I have tried in the last years to re-make the gardens as they might have been, and bring them back into sympathy with the great unchanging house. It is my dream that one day they will become again a place of fancies and conceits, where not only pleasure and peace can be found but a measure of surprise and mystery'. Every visitor – and there are 150,000 each year – will agree that she has succeeded in both her designs and her plantings.

ABOVE The splendid entrances to the Privy Garden have been trained and clipped as topiary tiers.

RIGHT Hoar frost on the standard honeysuckles in the Scented Garden. Camomile grows around the central sun-dial to further perfume the summer air.

King Henry's Hunting Lodge

Down a long muddy track in a wood near Odiham in Hampshire stands Nicholas Haslam's Gothic extravaganza. King Henry's Hunting Lodge was one of many rococo follies that Paulet St John built when he landscaped Dogmersfield Park in the 1760s. But the present harmony between house and garden is largely due to John Fowler, one of the founders of Colefax & Fowler, who bought King Henry's Hunting Lodge in 1948.

Fifty years ago, the garden was unmanaged oak and holly woodland with marshy, thin and sandy soil. Hitler's war had barely finished. It was a time of great deprivation and austerity and everyone longed for gaiety and colour. It is greatly to John Fowler's credit that he did not encircle his Gothic folly with drifts of gorgeously coloured azaleas from the nurseries of Bagshot and Knaphill. Instead, he turned to the baroque traditions of 18th-century France and Germany for inspiration, and created a formal

LEFT Statues and Versailles tubs fill the small terrace in front of the house and emphasize the formal setting laid out by John Fowler.

ABOVE The view along the main cross axis is beautifully symmetrical. Here, the ogee outline of the pavilion reflects the shape of the window's of the Hunting Lodge as shown in the photograph to the left.

setting which perfectly matches the theatrical dottiness of the Hunting Lodge and anchors it firmly in the wider woodland landscape that surrounds it.

King Henry's Hunting Lodge was originally intended to be seen from the far shore of Wilks Water, the lake at the bottom of the wood. Its three Gothic gables of warm red brick are reflected in the still water. John Fowler made the view down from the house to the water's edge and back the governing element of his design. There are cross-tensions and incidents on the way, but the garden emphasizes this one stupendous axis. Vines, climbing roses and *Magnolia grandiflora* adorn the walls of the house, but the view from the house is flowerless. Stand at the main door of the house and look down to the lake some 110m (120yd) below and only a progression of green shapes can be seen. Carefully clipped hornbeam hedges frame the view.

The walk down to the water's edge leads past obelisks of box and topiary bobbles, through white-painted drop-circle gates (the gateposts topped by slender pyramidal finials), and along a broad grass path with unmown edges. The lake is bordered by poplars and willows, an airy contrast to the dark shapes of the native woodland. Beyond the lake is a modern eye-catcher, a painted obelisk by Martin Newall which Nicholas Haslam brought here from Lady Juliet Duff's garden at Bulbridge House, Wilton.

The long rectangular lawn below the house is hedged on either side by clipped hornbeam stilts in the baroque style. Half way down, a strong transverse axis cuts across the lawn between two elegant, white-

ABOVE The brick Gothic arches of King Henry's Hunting Lodge as they were originally intended to be seen, reflected in Wilks Water.

painted fretwork summerhouses whose grace derives from their tall pointed roofs. One of the summerhouses is the 'sun' pavilion and the other is the 'shade' pavilion, according to their aspects. The Gothic windows of the 'sun' pavilion echo those of the house itself. A second lateral cross-axis opens out below the lawn and leads to the garden room, a spacious studio which acts as a summer drawing room. It over-

ABOVE The small formal garden in front of the Garden Room is entirely in scale. The unrestrained pink and white plantings that fill the box hedges are a striking contrast in this formal setting.

looks a box-edged quincunx planted with old-fashioned roses, fox-gloves and rosemary. The design is intimate and stylish.

Lines and angles, symmetry and formality are the essence of the garden at King Henry's Hunting Lodge. Every straight line is framed by matching features and terminates in an eye-catcher. Even the grav-elled path to the greenhouse passes between high hornbeam hedges and is lined with box topiaries in grey-and-brown painted tubs. But the garden also exemplifies the contrast between open and shut, motion and rest. There is a sense of movement leading away from the house, down the gentle slope towards the end of the lawn where it comes to rest at the edge of Wilks Water. Here the view opens out to reveal yet further inviting prospects. But, in con-trast, sit in one of the enchanting trellis pavilions and only the quiet symmetries of an enclosed garden can be seen.

When he died twenty years ago, John Fowler left King Henry's Hunting Lodge to the National Trust. Since 1979, when he became a tenant of the Trust, Nicholas Haslam – no less renowned as an interior designer

– has continued to maintain and improve the garden. He has respect-ed the hard landscape of the design, and it is only the plantings that change from year to year. Out came some of the discreet old roses, but they were replaced by modern lookalikes that flower all through the summer instead of just the once. Likewise, the standard of mainte-nance throughout the garden is exemplary: John Fowler could not have wished for a better successor at King Henry's Hunting Lodge, nor one in greater sympathy with his creative genius.

ABOVE The great lawn in front of the Lodge is contained within a double line of pleached limes.

OPPOSITE The benefits of symmetry and balance in garden design are clearly seen in this view from the Garden Room.

ADVENTUROUS
PLANTING

Butterstream

Jim Reynolds began gardening at Butterstream in about 1970, when he was still a student of archaeology at University College Dublin. He started by taking in a corner of a field on the family farm but over the intervening years the farm has got smaller and the garden has just continued to grow. There were originally three garden rooms, now there are nearly twenty.

The gardens at Butterstream are not connected to the house in any way; rather, they are set apart from the real world. There is a preferred sequence for visiting the gardens, which follows Jim's own progress as a gardener, but visitors are free to follow whatever course takes their fancy. The scale is at first intimate, almost modest: the planting is cottagey. Then each successive design becomes more expansive. The most recent addition – long canals that burn in the evening sun – is worthy of the grandest baroque palace in France or Germany.

Garden history and garden design have always been among Jim's enthusiasms. One of his earliest essays at Butterstream was the rose garden, whose thick box hedges, 1m (1yd) high, are conceived as a tribute to Renaissance Italy. They are intended to suggest an ancient garden that has been recently brought under control and filled with old roses. Not only does the high hedge create a feeling of age, it also hides the lanky stems of the roses. These include the old crimson hybrid perpetual 'Duke of Wellington', whose family lived at nearby Trim. The hedges are also underplanted with *Clematis viticella*, foxgloves and catmint, to extend the season of flower beyond midsummer.

Jim says that he gets his ideas from visiting other people's gardens, and from reading such writers as Penelope Hobhouse, Christopher Lloyd and Graham Thomas. He is not interested in plants as collection pieces, nor even for their historical associations, but he does try to preserve and use good plants that are unappreciated elsewhere, particularly old Irish cultivars like *Primula* 'Rowallane Rose' and 'Lissadell Pink'. Jim insists that plants at Butterstream have to have 'garden value': they must be good team-workers. Even though his garden is full of especially interesting and well-grown plants, it is the design of and use of colour that has always interested him the most. He

PREVIOUS PAGE Thick box hedging surrounds irises and Campanula lactiflora *in this part of the herbaceous garden, the best-known feature at Butterstream.*

OPPOSITE Hostas and ferns line the Butterstream which gives its name to the garden. Note the elegant Gothic bridge behind.

maintains that colour gardening is all about using your eyes: you should see what works in other gardens and art forms and employ the same principles in your own garden.

Jim's first essay in colour gardening was a little 'hot' garden of reds, oranges and yellows inspired by Mount Stewart in County Down. Purple cordylines, purple phormiums and *Robinia pseudacacia* 'Frisia' provide structure. Seasonal colour comes from daylilies, crocosmias, *Papaver orientalis*, red tiger lilies, golden rod, ligularias and sunflowers, and the brown sedge *Carex buchananii*.

The best known garden at Butterstream is the generously large herbaceous garden with borders as much as 8m (8¾yd) deep and predominantly composed of blues, mauves and yellows – 'boudoir colours'. Jim makes large groupings that are oval in shape and something between a drift and a clump. He also believes in the power of repetition: staple plants like delphiniums, *Campanula lactiflora* and the white willowherb *Epilobium angustifolium album* appear several times in a border to bind it together. He plants thickly – 'I hate gaps and bare earth' – and finds in consequence that there is no need to weed the borders until very late in the year. Annuals and biennials fill in the gaps where early flowerers have died back.

The climax of a visit to Butterstream is Jim's newest venture – two large Palladian pavilions approached under a portico which came from Lord Mornington's demolished house in Trim. These are substantial buildings, as large as the grandest of ballrooms, and their scale reflects Jim's confidence in his garden and its future. Behind each pavilion – but this can't be seen until you are actually inside, looking out – is a broad, straight canal, perhaps 45m (60yd) long, which ends in a cascade outside the window. Along the outsides of these splendid pavilions are double avenues of limes.

Jim says that all his gardens at Butterstream are intended to delight the senses and elicit an emotion-

OPPOSITE Notice how the colours blend from left to right, starting with the palest of lavateras and moving through stronger pinks to the brightest crimson penstemon.

BELOW Stately white spires of verbascum rise from a haze of pinks and blues: the essence of Butterstream's dreamy planting.

al response. There is no doubt that his latest development has the desired effect. It also marks a new phase in his personal career. In 1991, he resigned his job as an archaeologist working for the Irish government and – at some considerable financial risk – sought a new career as a self-employed garden designer. By sheer luck *The Irish Times* almost simultaneously asked him to write a regular gardening column. Soon he was making a better living than he could ever have expected as a civil servant. It is hard to guess just what he will do next: much of the family farm is now Jim's garden.

ABOVE This Doric summerhouse (swathed in Clematis orientalis*) faces a rustic one (heavy with* Rosa *'François Juranville') across the tennis lawn: 'the civilized man opposite the savage', says Jim Reynolds.*

RIGHT Jim Reynolds's earliest essay in colour gardening is a little 'hot' garden of reds, oranges and yellows. Ligularias and Robinia pseudacacia *'Frisia' provide structure: crocosmias and purple cordylines fill the foreground.*

Wave Hill

Wave Hill is a public garden and cultural centre on the edge of New York's Bronx: 11.3 hectares (28 acres) of gardens and woodlands overlooking the Hudson River. Theodore Roosevelt's family lived there in 1870-71 and Mark Twain leased the house thirty years later: the noise and energy of the wind in the trees 'thrills me and stirs me and uplifts me and makes me want to live for ever', he wrote. But most of the garden was laid out and planted by George W Perkins, a partner of J P Morgan, from 1903 onwards. Perkins graded and contoured the land, built terraces, opened up long vistas across the river, planted trees around the sweeping lawns and blended the landscaping with the natural beauty of the wild woodland. In 1960, the Perkins family deeded the estate to the City of New York which maintains it 'to foster connections between people and the natural world'. The garden is used by the public for horticultural education and enjoyment, and it is a rich environmental education resource for New York City school children.

The garden owes its present eminence to the energy and aesthetic gifts of its director of horticulture Marco Polo Stufano. He uses it as a teaching resource for horticultural history and for such special interests as herbs and their uses. Indeed, the Herb Garden displays herbs from all over the world that people have used for healing, religious practices, food, flavouring, colouring and ornament. The horticultural collections extend to 1200 genera, 3250 species and countless cultivars used with strong attention given to the aesthetics of gardening in a widely varied group of garden areas.

The formal Aquatic Garden is home to both hardy and tropical water lilies and other distinctive water plants. The sacred lotus plant of India is hardy in the New York area and flowers each summer. The periphery of the rectangular pool is planted with a collection of grasses which are especially attractive at the waterside and relate to the Monocot Garden which stands within the curve of a fine old pergola nearby. The Monocot Garden seeks to display the beauty and diversity of plants known as monocotyledons, including such important economic plants as grasses, cereals and bamboos and also the visually striking and exotic elephant ears, palms and bananas.

OVERLEAF Colour combinations are a particular strength of the garden at Wave Hill. The yellow of the achillea flowers is picked up by the young hydrangea heads, which turn to bright blue later in the summer.

OPPOSITE The stately spires of Salvia sclarea *var.* turkestanica *contrast with the airy white* Lychnis flos-jovis *f.* alba *in the cottage garden.*

BELOW This close-up of the pink-tinged bracts of Salvia sclarea *var.* turkestanica *shows the fine detailing of a member of the sage family that grows up to 1m (3ft) in height.*

ABOVE Troughs, infinitely variable in their size and shape, are filled with alpine plants to provide colour and interest almost throughout the year from earliest spring to late in the season.

LEFT Ferns, hostas, phlox, Heuchera 'Palace Purple' and summer-snowflakes Leucojum aestivum *are among the many herbaceous plants beautifully blended in this sheltered woodland glade.*

The Flower Garden, which is located within an enclosure of rustic fencing in front of the Greenhouse complex, is a mixture of formality and exuberant abandon. Despite its spectacular views of the Hudson River and Palisade rock formations, it is still a space conducive to introspection and reflection. Marco Polo Stufano intends the planting to resemble a 'glorified cottage garden' through the use of both heirloom plants and modern cultivars of perennials, annuals, shrubs and bulbs. The use of colour, both flowers and foliage, is given a great deal of consideration in the beds. Lavishly planted containers are massed in the centre of the space and positioned along the brick paths. A special feature of this garden, as well as others at Wave Hill, is the emphasis upon autumn. Plants such as salvias, small flowered dahlias, and nicotianas revel in the glorious days of September and October in New York.

Wave Hill's glasshouses are particularly impressive. Plants are housed according to their cultural requirements in a palm house, a tropical house, a succulent house and an Alpine house. The palm house is a splendid porticoed structure and has a notable display of South African bulbs.

Three greenhouses which fell into disrepair many years ago have been demolished leaving only their foundation walls. A herb garden has been built within one of these enclosures, while the second one has become home to many plants from warmer and drier parts of the world, including lavenders, rosemaries and the rice paper plant *Tetrapanax papyrifea*. The surviving low surrounding foundation walls provide the reflected warmth and protection from wind without which these plants would not survive typical winters. Within the third foundation, a small Alpine

BELOW The purple blooms of Iris germanica *and mass of yellow crucifers (woad) look quite vibrant in a late spring downpour.*

house has been built for these sparkling diminutive treasures from the mountains. Also within the surrounding walls is an arrangement of hypertufa troughs filled with still more gems from high places.

The Wild Garden is designed in the style inspired by the writings of the 19th-century English gardener William Robinson. Plants from all over the world are grown here in a natural way, to suggest that they arrived here and flourished without human intervention. Bulbs are a great feature in spring and equally important are drifts of such early-flowering herbaceous plants as hellebores and celandines, and the thistles, Californian poppies and ornamental grasses of summer. Wave Hill has also been actively involved in reclaiming 4 hectares (10 acres) of its own woodlands and meadows from invasive exotics and encouraging the regeneration of native species. Restoration and maintenance are the key to success. So, too, is education: when contemplating Wave Hill's message it is not difficult to see how the relationship between people and the natural world has been fostered and appreciated.

ABOVE The Monocot Garden and Aquatic Garden at Wave Hill. Tropical water plants are put out in summer here while the Monocot Garden seeks to display the beauty and diversity of plants known as monocotyledons. The grasses featured here are Miscanthus sinensis *'Zebrinus',* M. s. *'Strictus', and* Panicum virgatum.

Dillon

The best modern gardens combine strong formal design with interesting plants and good plantings. The artistry depends upon all three elements: few gardens have each in abundance. It is not unusual for the combination to be design-led, or colour-led, because these are disciplines that can be learned from other art forms, but it is unusual for an avowed plantsman to make a garden which is also full of challenging design features arranged to please the eye. Helen Dillon's garden in south Dublin is this happy exception. Helen is, above all, an unashamed passionate collector of plants. Her great achievement has been to make a garden where the plants look especially good in combinations, and where the garden is satisfying, even in winter, because of its strong design.

Helen Dillon collects plants and invariably faces the challenge of how to combine her cabinet of horticultural curiosities with her desire to make a satisfying garden. Collectors' gardens are often too full of busy labels and boring plants. She came to the conclusion that she needed rules to bring order out of chaos – principles to organize her plants so that the garden was more than a cacophony of plant names. She identified three ways of doing this. First, it is vital to

ABOVE White Japanese anemones soak up the heat at the front of the house.

RIGHT The 'cool' border dominated by the large Buddleia *'Nanho Blue'. The variegated leaves are of* Symphytum x uplandicum *'Variegatum'.*

have a fairly strict and formal design to create a strong framework for the plants and plantings. Second, it is essential to group plants by colour. Third, plants should be placed according to their cultural needs: peat beds for Ericaceae, sharp drainage for alpines, and shelter for shade-lovers, for example. Once these principles have been applied, you can accommodate and cultivate whatever new plant takes your fancy and enjoy the satisfaction of making a good garden too. But Helen insists that 'gardening is the organization of living, ever-changing organisms, and therefore must be an everlasting and ever-circling process of looking, thinking and looking again.'

Helen's house was built in the 1830s and the garden has been cultivated ever since. Most of the garden lies behind the house – less than 0.35 hectare (1 acre) in extent and with a soil that is light and alkaline. The house is perched above it, so the garden and its outlines can be well appreciated. The design centres on an all-but-rectangular lawn, tapered to make it look longer. The lawn is also the path down the middle of the main double borders. Because of its breadth, the visitor is tempted to move only slowly, and this in turn increases the sense of space that the whole garden enjoys. The borders alongside the lawn are divided to create a total of four long, rectangular beds: a silver and pastel-pink border; a blue border; a red border, and finally a bulb border which also has a patch for what Helen calls 'difficult pinks', meaning colours like magenta, rose-madder and Tyrian purple.

Helen believes that it is very important to put plants into ground where they will thrive. To this end, she is prepared to make special beds

ABOVE Helen Dillon's conservatory, most used for overwintering tender exotics, is given a formal setting which helps to connect its architecture to the garden.

to accommodate particular needs. For example, she has created a shady, lime-free bed for alkali haters. It supports such plants as the scarlet climber *Mitraria coccinea*, the stately *Paris polyphylla*, and *Meconopsis × sheldonii* 'Slieve Donard', the bluest of poppies. Likewise, Helen has made a gravel garden which suits such plants as the double orange perennial wallflower *Erysimum* 'Harpur Crewe' and the so-called strawberry-raspberry *Rubus illecebrosus*.

ABOVE Kniphofias (not-too-red-hot-pokers) and pale hemerocallis (daylilies) have been grouped together for their apricot and cream shades.

'For me, the plant always comes first. Every effort should be made to grow it well. Then comes a problem: how to place it so that it complements its neighbours. So I try to plant with colour in mind.' Unity in a plantsman's garden is provided by colour, not by the sheer variety of plants that flourish in an Irish climate. Helen begrudges repeating a plant because it then takes up space which could be used for something new. But she does like to use background foliage plants to pull her garden together at all seasons. They include the dainty grey-leaved *Artemisia* 'Powis Castle', *Heuchera* 'Palace Purple' and *Berberis thunbergii* 'Atropurpurea Nana'.

ABOVE The central lawn creates a sense of repose in a busy garden and acts as a spacious corridor between the red and blue borders.

LEFT Crimson dahlias Dahlia *'Bishop of Llandaff' give late-summer richness to the red borders: note the* Berberis thunbergii *'Atropurpurea Nana', one of Helen Dillon's background foliage plants which pull her garden together.*

DECORATION AND ORNAMENT

Little Sparta

Ian Hamilton Finlay's Little Sparta is widely considered Scotland's most interesting new garden for many years. Sir Roy Strong once wrote that, although he had not visited it, he never hesitated to assert that Little Sparta was the most original garden made in Britain since 1945. The fact that the garden is seldom open to the public and has been seen by few visitors makes this reputation all the more remarkable. But there is no doubting the extraordinary creativity that it expresses, nor its significant effect on garden owners all over the world.

Ian Hamilton Finlay is a poet, and a concrete poet at that, believing that the essence of any intellectual idea can be represented both in words and in other art forms. Little Sparta is his masterpiece: it combines sculptures, ornaments and artefacts into a single work of art which is greater than the sum of its parts. It is modelled on 18th-century antecedents, including Stowe and Stourhead (both conceived as intellectual experiences), but particularly on the garden at The Leasowes where the poet William Shenstone used inscribed commentaries to evoke an ideal classical world. At Little Sparta, the contrast between that ideal world and the world today enables Finlay to develop a political and social commentary. But the garden offers entertainment and laughter, as well as philosophical allusions and moral imperatives.

The house was originally known as Stonypath, but Finlay renamed it Little Sparta as part of a Five-year Hellenization Plan. The house itself – a windswept croft on an inhospitable moorland – was transformed by painting Doric pilasters across its face. Starting in the sunken front garden, there is a sequence for a tour around the garden. The message in the round pool is 'the sphere complements the circle', and as the garden is explored, there are ever more inscriptions to ponder: on paving, benches, column bases, and even on trees. They draw you into

PREVIOUS PAGE A golden head of the sun god, his forehead inscribed Apollon Terroriste.

OPPOSITE The glowering Pentland Hills are the backdrop is St Just's pronouncement on great tablets of stone: THE PRESENT ORDER IS THE DISORDER OF THE FUTURE.

BELOW Finlay changed Stonypath's name to Little Sparta as part of his Five-year Hellenization Plan.

Finlay's world, where philosophical and political themes combine: his preoccupations include the classical world, the 18th-century enlightenment, the French Revolution, the German romantic movement, the Second World War, and the subversive power of surrealism. The sea is a constant theme: stone models of fishing boats, submarines and an aircraft carrier fill the pools. War and the absurdity of war are perennial concerns: tanks and aircraft are our modern symbols of power, the false gods to whom we are in thrall. Two bronze tortoises have 'Panzer Leader' engraved upon their shells. Power and its abuse are constantly highlighted. Violence is mocked by a tombstone in front of a group of cherry trees which beseeches us to 'Bring Back the Birch'.

At the back of the house, the tempo quickens and the scale expands. Finlay knows how to use space well. The separate incidents are connected and divided by paths, vistas, plantings, and changes of texture. The banks of the Temple Pool in the original farmyard are strewn with classical masonry in the manner of the great German neo-classicist Karl Schinkel. Brick gate piers (their pineapple finials transmuted into hand grenades) lead through scrubby woodland to a stone pyramid: this is dedicated to Caspar David Friedrich, the high priest of German romantic painting who imbued his canvases with the power and grandeur of nature. Here, too, are neo-classical cut-outs of Daphne and Apollo in black and red and a stone grotto dedicated to Dido and Aeneas. A golden head of the sun god, his forehead inscribed *Apollon Terroriste*, rests at ground level in contemplation of a small pool.

ABOVE Finlay's grim sardonic humour mocks the violence of our times.

OPPOSITE The work of bees is evoked both in verse and stone.

Out in the open countryside again, with the glowering Pentland Hills as a backdrop, is St Just's portentous aphorism in classical lettering on great tablets of stone: THE PRESENT ORDER IS THE DISORDER OF THE FUTURE. Further up the hill there is the Hegel stile, inscribed: 'THESIS: fence. ANTHITHESIS: gate. SYNTHESIS: stile', and an injunction to 'SEE POUSSIN, HEAR LORRAIN'. This makes a connection not only to the French

HIVES THRU LEAVES
WINGS THRU WAVES

landscape painters but also to the classical world they reinvented. So, too, Dürer's monogram AD hanging from a tree puts one immediately in touch with the northern humanist renaissance. But the garden is not a book of allusions and quotations written in stone. Each object is a statement and each area develops an idea: they are each chapters of a commentary that builds up into a work of art in its own right.

Plants play a minor role in the garden. Nature and art are here undivided. Ian Hamilton Finlay belongs to the 18th century, when the materials of landscape were trees, grass, stone and water. Flowers and their colours are an irrelevance. Indeed, Finlay has remarked that horticulturists enter a neo-classical garden 'with the air of police conducting a weapon search'. The science of cultivation is limited to some experiments with unspectacular groundcover plants – astrantias, lamiums and hardy geraniums – as well as wild campanulas, speedwell, Welsh poppies and ferns. Although Little Sparta is not a gardened garden, it does reflect the changing seasons and celebrates the natural cycles of birth and death, love and tragedy. On the three square columns in the Henry Vaughan Walk are the sequence: 'The contem-

plation of death is an obscure melancholy walk ... An expiation on shadows and solitude ... But it leads unto life'.

When at last he was able to visit Little Sparta, Roy Strong reflected that 'no other garden has made me so aware of the poverty of context of all late 20th-century gardens, or made me give so much thought to the true meaning of my own garden and how I can best articulate it.' It is a fit reaction. Finlay's achievement has been to bring back the immediacy of classical art and its message. Little Sparta challenges us to put Greece and Rome at the heart of our own culture.

ABOVE Neo-classical cut-outs of Daphne and Apollo inhabit a wild woodland garden.

York Gate

Robin Spencer once summed up his garden at York Gate as 'an owner-made and maintained garden of particular interest to the plantsman, containing orchard with pool, an arbour, miniature pinetum, dell with stream, a folly, a nut walk, peony bed, iris borders, fern border, herb garden, summerhouse, alley, white and silver garden, two vegetable gardens, and pavement maze all within one acre.'

ABOVE This view of the White Garden from the kitchen windows focuses on the barley-sugar column at the end.

RIGHT The hexagonal rustic folly standing over a circular stone and gravel base is central to many of the best vistas within the garden.

All of which is absolutely true, but he omitted to mention the Japanese-style garden, the bog garden, a collection of bonsai, an Italianate loggia and several arbours. This is an astounding list of contents but it does not explain why York Gate has been described as one of the greatest post-war gardens in England. Nor does it convey how a garden with so much variety, ornament and incident should nevertheless feel open and uncramped.

Robin Spencer's parents moved to York Gate in 1951 and allowed him – then a teenager – free rein to design and develop it. His three abiding interests were gardening, design and collecting: and they have all come together with equal emphasis in the remarkable gardens of York Gate. He had an extraordinary ability to acquire artefacts and to use them for ornamental purposes. Almost any piece of stone or domestic article was something of

value to him. Spencer believed that, just as a room can absorb no end of furniture, so too a garden can take almost any amount of ornament, with the result that the only criticism which might be levelled at York Gate is that it is perhaps too busy and too fussy. But it is very much a garden of its times, and it is important to remember in these post-minimalist days, that the joy of garden-making in the 1970s (as with interior design) was the piling on of detail. But Spencer was selective in his choice, and his real interest was in the recycling of utilitarian objects – not just the troughs and sinks, which Yorkshire gardeners have collected for generations, but also such improbable artefacts as old stone grinders, industrial boilers and kitchen pans, which are used as bonsai containers The most surprising objects found their way into Spencer's garden and look exactly 'right' where he placed them.

Robin Spencer could never quite analyse the process by which he put an object in a particular place. One example of a successful place-ment is the wobbly column sundial at the end of the white border: imagine what the view from the house would be without that focal point. Likewise, one of the main axes down towards the folly leads out of a circular window in the potting shed and the view is crystallized by a white-painted utilitarian pump head beyond.

The scale of the garden is small and intimate, and yet this is used to create long vistas. The herb garden makes exquisite use of space: you would never guess from its photographs that it is less than 5m (5½yd) wide. The helter-skelters and globes of box are particularly noticeable and all are perfectly proportioned. The use of space everywhere is inge-nious and satisfying. Robin was also interested in the uses of stone, paving, setts, mill stones, cobbles and gravel, in all their different sizes and colours, and he had an unerring eye for form and texture.

Robin also collected plants. There is a tremendous variety at York Gate, but it is not the garden of a plantsman – rather, of someone who was fascinated by the infinite forms, colours and textures of plants and

LEFT A raised canal – long and remarkably narrow – offers all the design advantages of water and stone in a confined area.

OVERLEAF The proportions of the Herb Garden, seen here from the Doric loggia at one end, are near perfect.

the sheer variety they offered him for decorative purposes. He made especially good use of evergreens: the conifer collection is one of the high points of the garden. It includes a very fine *Picea smithiana*, a bristlecone pine *Pinus aristata* and a form of *Abies concolor* called 'Wattezii'. The ground beneath them has been surfaced with large, loose, round cobbles of more-or-less uniform colour and size, in homage to the Japanese tradition. A nearby wall is clothed with an extraordinary espaliered *Cedrus atlantica* only 1m (3ft) high, a triumph of training.

The planting concentrates upon autumn and winter effects. It is easy to have a good display in summer, and York Gate is no exception when its stupendous herbaceous plantings of irises and paeonies are in full flower. But it is in the winter that the flowers are appreciated the most, especially the hellebores, aconites and snowflakes, as well as the fern walk and two magnificent specimens of *Trachycarpus fortunei*, one of them 3m (10ft) high against the east wall of the house.

In 1981, Robin wrote 'I consider I am very lucky to be able to watch and tend what appears to be a comparatively mature garden which I have planted, and yet be only in comfortable middle age [he was then 47]; but the creative process never stops, each year has its project, and the layout is still evolving'. Alas, he died shortly afterwards. In due course, his mother bequeathed it to the Gardeners' Royal Benevolent Society. The house is now used for the Society's principal purpose of helping gardeners suffering from ill health and providing accommodation for them in their old age. Richard Staples is the head gardener, a very senior horticulturist: York Gate is in good hands.

ABOVE The parking area in front of the house has been inlaid with setts to create a circular maze.

OPPOSITE York Gate has a wonderful variety of decorative shapes and material: this path of gravel, setts and millstones runs down to the folly.

Cottesbrooke

Cottesbrooke is the garden with everything: a long drive through majestic parkland, a classical bridge, a fabulously pretty house, lakes, waterfalls, bluebell woods, rhododendrons, acres of daffodils, 34 cultivars of snowdrop, half-a-dozen garden rooms, Scheemakers' statues from Stowe, an armillary garden, pergolas, *allées*, three-hundred-year-old cedars, new developments every year, immaculate maintenance, a gifted owner, an able head gardener, plants a-plenty, and the signatures of Geoffrey Jellicoe and Sylvia Crowe among the designers who have helped to develop it.

Cottesbrooke Hall itself is one of the loveliest houses in England: some say that it was the model for Jane Austen's Mansfield Park. It was built in the reign of Queen Anne on a straight axis with the Saxon tower of Brixworth Church, some 5km (3 miles) to the south. The park was landscaped in the 18th century, but the formal designs, which are the glory of the garden at Cottesbrooke, date from the 1930s. Geoffrey Jellicoe and Sylvia Crowe are the two big names associated with the lay-out, but many of the plantings and all the latest improvements are the work of the present owner John Macdonald-Buchanan and his wife.

The formal garden in front of the house was laid out by Jellicoe in 1938 and is enclosed by two pavilions connected to the house by wings. Cones of yew and thick parterres planted with white 'Pascali' roses provide the structure to this garden: each quarter centres on a classical statue – Venus, Diana, Hermes and Eros. In summer, the urns and pots are filled with exotic plantings of agapanthus and conservatory plants.

The heart of the garden is the Pool Garden, once full of Edwardian roses, but now a spacious walled garden with a circular sunken lily-pool at the centre. Fine climbing roses and shrubs cover the walls, but the best way to appreciate the spirit of the place is to sit in the sheltered loggia designed by Sylvia Crowe where the following verse is engraved on the wall:

> *The Kiss of the sun for Pardon,*
> *The song of the Birds for mirth,*
> *One is nearer God's heart in a garden*
> *Than anywhere else on earth.*

ABOVE A splendid Fuchsia *'Thalia' arches above a procumbent underplanting of* Fuchsia *'Marinka'.*

OPPOSITE This view across the balustrade at the edge of the forecourt runs down a broad new avenue to a woodland cut 1.5km (1 mile) away.

Crowe's loggia is also the best place to contemplate the longest and finest of the axes which are such a feature of the pleasure gardens at Cottesbrooke. It runs from the lily pool through the tall gates in the far wall (elegant stone hounds atop the pillars) and along a pleached lime avenue to a handsome lead statue of a Roman gladiator and beyond to a long avenue of London planes. The transition from 20th-century plantsmanship to 17th-century formality is nothing short of perfect.

Along the outer edge of the Pool Garden is the long double herbaceous border known as the Terrace Border, a magnificent example of colour planting. A few shrubs give it structure, but the most architectural plantings are four groups of yuccas which mark the corners of three cross-axes. Half-hardies like cannas and dahlias prolong the season. At the end of the border is the new formal rose garden called the Philosopher's Garden: its beds of 'Nathalie Nypels' surround central trellis-work pyramids (made by the estate carpenter) swathed in 'Mme Isaac Pereire'. Cottesbrooke is known too for its summer plantings

ABOVE Rich herbaceous plantings including delphiniums, mallows, day lilies, and tender shrubs against the wall, are a feature of Cottesbrooke.

OPPOSITE Scheemakers' statues were bought by John Macdonald-Buchanan's grandparents in the original Stowe auction in the 1890s.

OVERLEAF The urns in the forecourt are filled with Fuchsia 'Thalia', *variegated pelargoniums and* Argyranthemum 'Mary Wootton'.

throughout the garden of tender plants in urns and vases. Fuchsias are a speciality, while the orange foxglove cousin *Isoplexis canariensis* is one of the many rare plants that are brought together in beautiful and satisfying combinations.

John Macdonald-Buchanan understands the need for firm design and for every axis to have a strong focal point. The urns which provide a focus for the Terrace Garden and for the nearby Dilemma Garden (its design includes two 'horns') are copies of the urns on the roof of the house, which were themselves designed in the 1930s by Lord Gerald Wellesley, the architect Duke of Wellington. When they needed replacement, two extra copies were made for the garden.

Cottesbrooke is wonderfully rich in statues. As well as the gladiator in the Spinney Garden, there is a handsome lead statue of Diana the Huntress in the Pool Garden, and a sandstone statue of Charles I's favourite dwarf Sir John Hudson. But pride of place must go to the four statues by Peter Scheemakers, the Dutch sculptor who made his living in England in the mid-18th century. They are four of the worthies made for a temple at Stowe: copies of Socrates, Lycurgus, Epaminondas and Homer have recently been made and used in the restoration of Stowe's landscape, but the originals remain at Cottesbrooke. They were bought by John Macdonald-Buchanan's grandparents in the original Stowe auction in the 1890s.

But not everything at Cottesbrooke is redolent of 18th-century grandeur or Edwardian opulence. Pass through the gate erected in memory of John Macdonald-Buchanan's mother, Lady Macdonald-Buchanan, who was the real creator of the whole garden. Walk across the park where a woodland garden lies hidden in a valley, and here the banks of a stream are richly planted with water irises, candelabra primulas, rheums and gunnera. At one end, in the Wild Garden, is a large collection of *Galanthus* from the famous galanthophile Lady Beatrix Stanley who lived at nearby Sibbertoft: this part of the garden is open one Sunday every year just for its snowdrops. From snowdrops to Scheemakers, Cottesbrooke is indeed the garden with everything.

ABOVE The banks of the stream in the Woodland Garden are lined with candelabra primulas in late May.

ABOVE The view across the Pool Garden through the tall Dog Gates, along a pleached lime avenue. The limes lead to a statue of a Roman gladiator and beyond to a long avenue of London planes.

LEFT Handsome clumps of yuccas add both structure and body to the Terrace Border.

WILDER GARDENS

Great Dixter

PREVIOUS PAGE Hawkbit and ox-eye daisies: a narrow mown path shows wildflower meadows to their best.

OPPOSITE 'Emperor' daffodils have naturalized in their thousands in the orchard at Great Dixter.

BELOW Wild primroses Primula vulgaris *and wood anemones* Anemone nemorosa *will quickly naturalize in light shade.*

Christopher Lloyd has written so eloquently and prolifically about the principles and practices of meadow gardening that, even if he had never penned a word on any other aspect of ornamental horticulture, he would be established as a great apostle of the charming and relaxed art form that he sometimes refers to as 'tapestry gardening'. Of course, not everyone appreciates his achievement: even after so many years of preaching the gospel, 'your lawns are weedy' is the perennial refrain of certain visitors to his garden. Lean over his front gate in July, when the meadows are at their most grassy, and it may not be immediately obvious to see why Great Dixter is such a famous garden, but remember that meadow gardening is only one of many horticultural art forms mastered by this remarkable pioneer.

Lloyd is certain that untidiness in a garden does not matter, as long as the owner is aware of it and does not mind it himself. Once the volume of work required is more than he is willing to give, the garden becomes a burden, and gardening a chore. For many years, Lloyd has shown how to halve the labour put into a garden, without detracting from the pleasures and rewards. A particular joy of gardening in rough grass is that it can be given as much or as little attention as is desired: the only essential is to cut and collect the grass three times a year. This explains why the view over the entrance gate to Dixter in high summer appears so unkempt: nothing can be cut until late July at the earliest, so that all the late flowerers have the opportunity to ripen their seed and increase their race. Lloyd resists the temptation

ABOVE By planting just one or two daffodil cultivars, a more natural effect is achieved.

to cut his grass earlier, even though its rankness may offend his visitors. And, of course, he has the pleasure of knowing that the untidiness is deliberate and perfectly justifiable.

Christopher Lloyd's parents laid out the garden at Great Dixter just before the First World War. When the upper moat was drained, Christopher's mother (her maiden name was Daisy Field) began a 'Botticelli garden' inspired by the painter's 'Primavera'. She planted snowflakes *Leucojum aestivum*, polyanthus, the native Lent lily *Narcissus pseudonarcissus*, Dutch crocuses, *Fritillaria meleagris* and

Orchis mascula: all have flourished and multiplied over the years. Indeed, the native daffodils and fritillaries have spread to other parts of the garden. There are now several colonies of the snakeshead fritillary, both the chequered purple species and the albino form. In the 1930s, Mrs Lloyd added two more local species of orchid, the green-winged *Orchis morio* and the spotted *Dactylorhiza fuchsii*. They, too, have naturalized in their thousands: her son once counted 37 specimens of the spotted orchid in one corner of rough grass. Indeed, so rare have modern methods of agriculture made them in this part of Sussex that the Lloyds can fairly claim to have helped to conserve these orchids. 'This is what is meant by naturalizing plants … it creates a home for many plants that modern systems of farming have made quite rare in the wild.'

The essence of meadow gardening is to let the native mixture of grasses and flowers provide a tapestry of background colour and add to them as you see fit. The season at Dixter is long. It starts in January or February with the first snowdrops and winter crocuses, especially the rich orange *Crocus flavus* ssp. *flavus*, *C. chrysanthus* and the slender mauve *C. tommasinianus*. They are followed by the Lent lilies and fat Dutch hybrid crocuses in March, together with the pretty alpine dog-tooth violet *Erythronium dens-canis* whose purple-pink flowers rise above chocolate-spotted leaves. Next come more daffodils, which compete well with grass in their natural habitat. Moreover, the growing grasses hide their ugly dying leaves, which makes it one of the best ways to grow narcissus. For a better and more natural effect, plant just one cultivar and avoid

BELOW Modern agriculture endangers many orchids, including the Dactylorhiza fuchsii *which flourish among hawkbit at Great Dixter.*

ABOVE The green-winged orchid Orchis morio *has deep purple flowers and occurs naturally in grasslands throughout Europe.*

the cheap daffodil mixtures that are offered for naturalizing. April also brings the wood anemones (which vary considerably in their colour, shape and size) and the pretty blue *A. apennina*.

After the fritillaries (they are still surprisingly cheap to buy, but do need heavy, damp soil) come the elegant, blue-flowered *Camassia quamash*, which are a splendid sight at Dixter. Magenta-flowered *Gladiolus byzantinus* throw shafts of bright magenta among the lengthening grasses in early summer, when the native buttercups *Ranunculus acris* and *R. bulbosus* take over as the principal sources of colour, together with ox-eye daisies and red clover. Blue meadow cranesbill *Geranium pratense* and yellow hawkbit *Leontodon autumnalis* are the mainstays of high summer, and the hawkbit responds to the mowing in July/August by flowering again in autumn with the colchicums and autumn crocuses *C. speciosus* and *C. nudiflorus*.

Christopher Lloyd recommends three cuts: one at the end of July, after everything has seeded, to tidy it up. The second, at the end of August, creates a smooth green background for the autumn bulbs. The turf then receives its last cut in late October or early November, so that snowdrops and crocuses can flower against short-cropped grass in winter. He also suggests starting meadow plantings at the top of a lawn, because the seeds will bounce down the slope and spread more quickly downhill than up. It is essential to add no fertilizers: grasses always benefit more from such nourishment than the bulbs and flowers on which the flowery meadow depends. In fact, it is best to start with an established lawn, so that only the finest grasses are in competition with the colourful plants. To convert an area of longer grass into a wild-flower meadow, it is usually best to mow it to a fine turf for a year before doing so.

Christopher Lloyd adds two further pieces of wisdom. First, the flower proportions differ greatly from year to year: each season brings better growth for some species than others and so the successes differ. Second, in general, the more open and unshaded the meadow, the richer and more varied the species it will support. But go to Dixter and see this art practised to perfection. And remember that meadow gardening is only one of many lessons that this great garden teaches.

ABOVE The blue spikes of Camassia quamash *flourish among the wild cow parsley* Anthriscus sylvestris.

Winkworth Arboretum

Dr Wilfred Fox bought the 40-hectare (100-acre) site of Winkworth Farm in 1938, attracted by 'the remarkable beauty of the valley, a valley quite unspoiled, of pastoral and wooded character'. He wanted to plant a large number of trees and to plant them in drifts, to suggest a natural stand, so his first plantings were of maples, a genus of which he was particularly fond. Among the most successful have been *Acer rubrum*, *A. grosseri* var. *hersii* and *A. trautvetteri*, all of them spectacularly coloured yellow or red in autumn and, in the case of *A. trautvetteri*, just as colourful when its new leaves issue in spring. Fox also planted a drift of some one hundred Japanese maples, all forms, cultivars and hybrids of *Acer palmatum* and *A. japonicum*. As a result, by the time of his death in 1962, Winkworth was well established as one of the leading modern arboreta in England.

Dr Fox had a passion for trees and was the founder of the Roads Beautifying Committee. This organization was responsible for vast plantations of ornamental trees and shrubs along many main roads in the south of England. Because motorists travel at speed, large numbers of a single tree have to be planted to make any impact. One abiding legacy of the committee's work are the miles of Surrey roadsides planted with the pink Japanese cherry 'Kanzan'. Fox believed that by planting on a large scale, the native landscape could be ignored: the plantings took over and *became* the landscape. It was a fashionable viewpoint at the time, and one which he applied at

ABOVE *The startlingly amber-yellow berries of* Sorbus *'Joseph Rock' are quite distinctive.*

RIGHT *Cedars and Japanese maples provide a striking background for this unique multi-stemmed planting.*

Winkworth. It is for posterity – us – to judge whether his theories have worked out well in practice.

It was not quite true to describe the valley as 'quite unspoiled' in 1936. It had already been dammed to make two artificial lakes: the lower is called Phillimore Lake and the upper one Rowes Flashe Lake. Between them lies a marshy area known as the wetlands, where *Gunnera manicata* has naturalized and spread over as much as 0.8 hectares (2 acres): it fills the valley bottom with a jungly sense of scale.

It was on the hillside above these two artificial lakes that Dr Fox made his arboretum. The lower reaches of the valley sides were meadowland, and still have an openness, which enhances the views from the lakeside up to the upper slopes, which were always woodland. Fox connected the lakes with the woods above by a steep climb up the azalea steps where hundreds of Kurume azaleas (some now old enough to be encrusted with lichens) are backed by plantings on both sides of maples, magnolias and eucryphias: the effect is stunning in late spring.

ABOVE The leaves of Liquidambar styraciflua *litter the ground for weeks on end, holding their glorious colours until early winter.*

RIGHT The rich red Acer palmatum *'Osakazuki' is one of the best for autumn colours in the azalea glade at Winkworth.*

At the top, the native species on this thin Surrey soil (a slice of the lower greensand) are beech, birch, oak and Scots pine. Primroses brighten the woodland in spring later becoming a vast expanse of wild bluebells. Within the woodland are splendid collections of sorbus (another genus in which Dr Fox was particularly interested), mahonias, amelanchiers, hollies and rhododendrons.

Winkworth is a true arboretum in the sense that it has a large collection of full-sized trees planted liberally over a large area. Many of the plantings are now in their prime. The acres of red oak, *Nyssa sylvestris* and *Liquidambar styraciflua* are quite spectacular in autumn. These last are especially striking because they hold on to their dying leaves for weeks on end, so that the colours intensify through yellow, orange, crimson and purple. Does their colour give the English a taste of the fall in New England? Opinions differ. At times it is certainly possible to imagine walking through the forests of Virginia or New York, but even on the scale of Wilfred Fox's plantings there is a feeling that they are no more genuine than the miles of pink Japanese cherries encountered in springtime on the journey to the arboretum. There is always that credibility gap when simulating the naturalization of exotic species.

ABOVE The collection of sorbus species and cultivars at Winkworth is one of the largest in the world.

OPPOSITE Native birches Betula pendula *are already turning yellow against the conifers above Rowes Flashe Lake. But the wild alders* Alnus glutinosa *remain green until late November.*

LEFT The pink-berried form of Sorbus hupehensis *sometimes carries its fruit throughout the winter: no one knows why they are unattractive to birds.*

Carpeted in flowers

OPPOSITE The old apple orchard is absolutely carpeted with mixed daffodils and Anemone blanda *in both its blue and white forms.*

BELOW Blue grape hyacinths surrounded by the most beautiful and fleeting species of ranunculus, common celandines.

There is much to be said for seeing what grows well for you and then planting lots of it. The owners of this family house in the Thames Valley have discovered that it is bulbs that do best for them on their well-drained, hungry soil, despite a régime which they describe as 'benign neglect'. The truth is that the family is strongly committed to the garden: the owners respect what they have inherited and seek to maintain it, but they also hope to improve the garden and, if possible, to restore some of the features that once gave it greater grandeur.

The bulbs flourish, so the owners regularly add to their numbers to supplement the natural increase which comes with the years. Grass is not cut until the bulbs have finished their annual growth and the leaves have died down for the summer. Where appropriate, they are mulched and fertilized with natural leaf-mould, but fallen leaves are cleared from the banks where the earliest snowdrops and aconites bloom, so that their late-winter splendour can be more easily enjoyed. The owners are careful to prune trees which shelter bulbs so that light reaches in and enables them to grow.

Bulbs are remarkably good value. Given the right encouragement, most will flourish and increase indefinitely. Individual bulbs form clumps of many and, if you are lucky, they seed themselves around as well. People do not always remember just how useful bulbs are in the garden. Most flower early in spring, long before the herbaceous garden

gets under way. It is all too easy to forget in high summer just how much pleasure there is to be gained from the earliest snowdrops, crocuses and aconites. They are subsequently followed at this Thames Valley garden by a wide and varied selection of bulbs: daffodils, muscari, celandines, anemones, ornithogalums, snakeshead fritillaries and the yellow form of crown imperial, *Fritillaria imperialis* 'Maxima Lutea'. Autumn then sees hundreds of naturalized cyclamen growing around an old chestnut near the house, as well as colchicums and autumn-flowering crocuses.

Gardens build up over many generations. Features linger long after their place in the scheme of things has been forgotten. Restoring an old family garden is often an exercise in detective-work and garden archaeology. To one side of the house is a circle of yew trees around a small mound. It appears on a map of the mid-18th century, and probably dates back a further two centuries, the last relic of a renaissance formal garden. Along one side is a younger row of yew trees: they probably represent an attempt to Tudorize the garden a hundred years ago.

In addition to its wild plantings, the garden also has elements of a romantic landscape, with its shapely contoured lake, wooded mound, vast specimen conifers and evergreen shrubberies. These last two are certainly Victorian, whereas the lake is at least fifty years older, and the mound (a sheet of aconites in spring) may even date back as far as the 16th century.

The handsome orchard to the south of the house is probably 19th-century. Daffodils and narcissi are naturalized here in their thousands, but the apple trees have begun to die out. The owners have therefore interplanted them with other types of tree: crataegus, sorbus, young holm oaks and the mahogany-bark *Prunus serrula*. This means not only that a small arboretum is now developing within the orchard, but also that the charm of bulbs naturalized in grass will be preserved for many years to come.

LEFT Snakeshead fritillaries Fritillaria meleagris *are a speciality of the Thames Valley: here they are starting to spread and naturalize.*

OVERLEAF Narcissus poeticus *var.* recurvus, *the old pheasant-eye narcissi, flourish in grassy meadows among blue and white anemones.*

Titoki Point

Gordon Collier's woodland garden at Titoki Point on New Zealand's North Island is quite remarkable: not only has he created the garden from scratch but he also planted the woodland in which it nestles. His family has farmed here for more than a century, and his father gave him 2.5 hectares (6 acres) on which to build his house when he married in 1965. There was nothing on the site at that time except for some sequoias, which were planted in 1923, and a few ancient *Alectryon excelsus*, the titoki trees from which Gordon's house takes its name. Now there is 1 hectare (2½ acres) of intensely planted woodland garden while the remaining 1.4 hectares (3½ acres) are an arboretum. One interesting effect of this planting is that, whereas in 1965 many degrees of winter frost were quite normal, and the garden together with its wooded slopes are now almost frost-free, and this enables Gordon to grow an impressive range of interesting plants.

Gordon is one of the kingpins of New Zealand gardening, chairman of the great rhododendron gardens at Pukeiti, and a vice-president of the International Dendrology Society. His international friendships have benefited his garden too. Titoki Point has rare species of pines collected in Mexico by the late Sir Harold Hillier, half-a-dozen specimens of *Rhododendron macabeanum* from seed collected in Assam, as well as a splendid collection of native New Zealand plants, all of which qualify on merit for their place in the garden. He chooses and places his plants mainly for their shapes and form: many are evergreen and are seldom seen in cultivation. Six of the

ABOVE The walkway through the bog garden passes by this stupendous specimen of Dicksonia fibrosa, *whose dying fronds form a protective skirt.*

OPPOSITE A simple timber summerhouse stands on the edge of the bog garden, surrounded by jungly leaves of tree ferns and kalopanax.

nine species of gunnera in the garden are New Zealand natives, as are all three dicksonia tree ferns: the slender *Dicksonia squarrosa*, the prostrate *D. lanata* and the distinctive *D. fibrosa* whose old fronds form a protective skirt around the trunk. And the magnificent *Cyathea dealbata*, one of New Zealand's national emblems, germinates spontaneously on shady banks.

Titoki Point is built high above a valley, at an altitude of 470m (1,500ft). Thirty-three kilometres (20 miles) to the north lies the snow-capped cone of the active volcano Mount Ruapehu, some 2,797m (9,175ft) high. The small garden at the front of the house has a level lawn, hedged around with *Teucrium fruticans*, and a splendid specimen of *Elaeagnus angustifolia* which frames the view of the volcano. The main garden lies down a steep slope to the west. The soil is heavy clay, except for the area which is now a bog garden, where a natural spring has created a rich accumulation of peaty soil. Rainfall is moderate, about 1m (40in) a year, but it falls in every month and this accounts for the natural luxuriance of the vegetation. The whole garden glows with lush good health. The path down the valley side runs past rhododendrons, camellias, clipped cones of box and a rich mixture of underplantings, especially hostas, ferns and day-lilies. But it is the bog garden, down in its peaty hollow, that is the best known feature of the garden. It lies beyond an avenue of weeping maples, edged with snow-drops and hellebores.

Native plants are an essential part of the design of the garden at Titoki Point, particularly *Cordyline australis*, an unlikely member of the lily family, and the gawky, lanky *Pseudopanax crassifolius*. The garden is seen at its best in late October, when the boggy bowl is bright with kingcups, irises and drifts of candelabra primulas. Later in the year, by early December, large patches of native renga lilies *Arthropodium cirratum* are in flower, while the giant Himalayan lilies *Cardiocrinum giganteum* are usually at their peak in time for Christmas. But it is the evergreen structure provided by the introduced

LEFT This strikingly green composition is on the edge of the bog garden. The spiky foliage of purple phormium, bamboos and irises dramatically contrast with the softer fronds of ferns, the round leaves of primulas and the elegantly drooping leaves of Hakonechloa macra *'Aureola'.*

native trees and shrubs which carries the garden over into autumn and winter. Sometimes it is almost impossible to believe that quite so much variety of plants and such a mature woodland garden have been created in just over thirty years. But they have, and the fame of Titoki Point is proof that Gordon Collier's fine achievement is recognized throughout the gardening world.

ABOVE Arum lilies, Zantedeschia aethiopica, *flower for weeks on end in early summer and thrive in the moist frost-free conditions.*

RIGHT The pool at the centre of the bog garden is fringed with irises, hostas, astilbes and many different species of candelabra primulas. The protecting hillside behind the pool is thick with evergreen trees and shrubs.

ROMANTIC GARDENS

Gresgarth Hall

Mark and Arabella Lennox-Boyd bought Gresgarth Hall near Lancaster in 1978. Mark was to become the Member of Parliament for nearby Morecambe and Lonsdale and had grown up at Ince Castle in Cornwall where his mother Lady Boyd of Merton built a remarkable collection of rare plants. Arabella is Italian, a professional landscape designer, with all the invention and flair of her native race. She has a wonderful eye for structure, line and colour. Arabella is an avid plantswoman and plant collector.

Gresgarth's original pele tower was revamped as a Norman-Gothic hybrid in Victorian times. Opinions are divided as to its architectural merits, but most visitors are charmed by its handsome windows and busy roofs. The estate runs to 56 hectares (138 acres), but only about

PREVIOUS PAGE The valley gives a glorious view of grandeur and space to both the house and gardens.

OPPOSITE The border on the edge of the lake is luxuriantly planted with drifts of candelabra primroses, ferns, rhododendrons and irises in spring.

BELOW The Lennox-Boyds extended the lake below the house so that now it seems to fill the whole valley.

BELOW Old roses like 'Complicata' (behind) and 'Fritz Nobis' (in front) are allowed to tumble over a flowery meadow of ox-eye daisies and clover.

4 hectares (10 acres) have been developed as gardens: the rest is parkland and woodland. The valley, which stretches up behind the house, is designated a Site of Special Scientific Interest for its rare mosses and liverworts. Through it runs a fast-flowing river, the Artle Beck, which comes off the fell behind and moves across the valley from one side to the other next to the house, giving the garden a glorious sense of grandeur and space. Springs are everywhere, and a great variety of soils which, together with the steep banks of the valley, make for an infinite number of micro-habitats in the fast-evolving garden.

A rugged stone boar guards the approach, which has parterres of the Lennox-Boyds' initials M and A on either side of the front door. The main formal gardens lie to the side of the house. Here there are terraces elegantly laid out with octagonal platforms, angled staircases and neat box edgings. The sundial was designed by Mark: it has two faces which tell the time accurately throughout the year. Much of the planting uses white flowers: *Daphne mezereum* 'Album', philadelphus, santolina and variegated hollies clipped as four-sided pyramids. *Clematis* 'Duchess of Edinburgh' and *C.* 'Henryi' grow against the retaining wall. Here and throughout the garden are magnificent hellebores, all the best modern cultivars from the leading hellebore breeders in Britain, Helen Ballard, Elizabeth Strangman, and Will McLewin in Cheshire.

A recent addition is the rectangular mosaic garden, edged by a long astral pavement with the star signs of the Lennox-Boyds. The design is most intricately worked in oval pebbles of many colours and sizes – and very beautiful. The surrounding borders are all in yellow and orange: rudbeckias, *Euphorbia dulcis* 'Chameleon', and annual sunflowers. The mosaic garden leads to the main herbaceous border, planted in pastel

shades and designed to flower from April to October – ending with a splendid show of Michaelmas daisies. Finally, there is a luminous white border, brilliantly effective on a long summer evening.

The terraces run down to the lake, which the Lennox-Boyds' have doubled in size. The damp border on its far side has glorious blue meconopsis, candelabra primulas in vast drifts, gunneras for late sum-

ABOVE The stylish bridge across the Artle Beck is best seen from this belvedere. Perched above the river's bank, it is swathed with old-fashioned rambling roses.

mer effect and both species of *Lysichiton*. A handsome bridge crosses the river to a long woodland garden that stretches along the valley bottom for about 400m (¼ mile). The dominant species is English oak but there are also remnants of a Victorian planting of sequoias and wellingtonias. The principal underplanting is of the winter-flowering witch hazels – *Hamamelis* 'Pallida', *H.* 'Diane', and many new cultivars.

By the water's edge, Arabella has re-erected a tower that formed part of her 'Ninfa' exhibit at the Chelsea Flower Show some years ago. The hillside across the river is laid out with an extensive collection of young rhododendrons. There are also a large number of magnolia forms and hybrids, an avenue of filberts and cobs along the outside of the walled garden, and a substantial group of the different cultivars of lilac. Micro-habitats support some surprisingly tender plants: *Embothrium coccineum*, *Drimys lanceolata*, and *Olearia scillonensis* all grow out in the open, as does the sweet-scented *Daphne bholua*, which is even beginning to seed around. Among the rarest plants are a fine young *Emmenopterys henryi*, micropropagated by Kew. Lilies also flourish especially well in this part of the garden, particularly the tall white *Cardiocrinum yunnanense*.

ABOVE Honeysuckles, lavender and the climbing rose 'Iceberg' are among the many pale-coloured plants that flower exuberantly on the terraces below the house.

OPPOSITE The dark Camassia esculenta *is one of the most striking of the wildflower plantings across the river.*

But it is above all the energy and the scale of Arabella Lennox-Boyd's endeavours that create the greatest impression. Mark and Arabella have successfully combined good design with thorough plantsmanship and a fine eye for decoration in a uniquely romantic natural setting. There can be no doubt that they are making one of the greatest gardens of modern times at Gresgarth.

Long Hall

OPPOSITE Yellow, pineapple-scented Cytisus battandieri *frames a view of Susannah Yeatman-Biggs' red border. There is a fine upright dark red berberis on the left-hand corner.*

BELOW The airy white Crambe maritima *contrasts well with the sturdy blue spikes of delphiniums.*

Long Hall is a substantial house in Wiltshire's Wylye valley: its origins are timber-framed and medieval but it has been enlarged and modernized so often over the years that its façade is now elegantly 18th-century. Originally it was known as Lower Farm but the Yeatman-Biggs gentrified the name when they acquired it in the 1860s as an addition to their Stockton estate. It now extends to 260 hectares (1 aquare mile), which Nicholas Yeatman-Biggs farms enthusiastically. But the soil in the garden, and on much of the farm, is thin and chalky.

Much of the romance of this garden lies in the fact that generations of Yeatman-Biggs have laboured here. Nicholas's wife Susannah has delved deep into the history of the garden to discover what each generation has contributed to its development. For example, Nicholas's great-grandfather planted nine Irish yews along the edge of the courtyard on the southern side of the house after he inherited Stockton in 1898. The garden also owes much to Nicholas's grandmother who lived at Long Hall from 1920 until 1972. She was a most energetic plantswoman and it was she who planted the luxuriant yew hedges that give the garden its structure. She also planted the hellebores and Madonna lilies along the cob walk leading from the main garden – 'a straight crib from Gertrude Jekyll', says Susannah.

Susannah took over in 1973. The great influences on her style of gardening have been Gertrude Jekyll (and indeed the whole English school of colour gardening) and the historian Alicia Amherst, who was the first person to pull the story of English gardening together into a proper historical account. Then there is the watercolourist George Elgood: one of Susannah's plantings, of sunflowers and lilies, comes straight from an Elgood painting. But it was a visit to the Berkeleys at Spetchley Park in her native Worcestershire that gave Susannah the impe-

tus to get on top of the garden. John Berkeley had started to restore the garden made famous by his great-aunt Ellen Willmott: the outcome inspired Susannah to start work at Long Hall.

The front door is flanked by laburnums grown in tubs. To one side, outside the kitchen and scullery windows, is a 'humpy' garden carved out of old holly trees and overgrown box, relics of a gloomy Victorian shrubbery. Walk across the turning circle and into the garden proper, and just over the garden wall is the parish church. There is a wonderful harmony between Long Hall and the church, as if the garden embraces them both. The bed in front of the boundary wall has been turned into an 'ecclesiastical' border. All its incumbents were chosen for their associations with members of the clergy: they include bishop's breeches (*Acanthus spinosus*), monkshood (*Aconitum napellus*), and the fine white 'Rambling Rector' rose. Nicholas Yeatman-Biggs' grandmother has also left her legacy in this warm, south-facing corner of the garden: a handsome tree of *Staphylea pinnata* and a vast *Cornus mas*, whose limbs have become contorted and interwoven over the years.

The house looks down over a lawn that runs 100m (110yd) to the south. Half way along is an old apple orchard, which has been interplanted with walnuts, limes and catalpas, and underplanted with such bulbs as *Crocus tommasinianus*, daffodils and cyclamen. But most of the action is off to the side, including the extensive herbaceous plantings in distinct colour combinations. The yellow garden is entered by an arch with yew peacocks on top. Further on are the pink and white borders. The grey-leaved form of *Buddleja alternifolia*, known as 'Argentea', is here – an ancient gnarled plant – and a weeping standard of the famous old rambling rose 'Excelsa', which sets it off. *Rosa gallica* 'Officinalis' contrasts with the lime-green flowers of a thalictrum, and there is a lovely combination of airy white *Crambe maritima* and blue delphiniums around the plum-bloom leaves of *Rosa glauca* in early summer. To one side is a vast medlar, an amazing specimen whose sweeping limbs have rooted over a huge area.

A clever design feature employed here and throughout the garden are a few shrubs that are planted right at the edge of borders, rather than being graded according to their height and planted further back. Purple elders and red-leaved berberis receive this treatment: the effect is to bring the border's edge closer, intensifying the sense of rich colour.

PREVIOUS PAGE Evening light throws its shadows across the long lawn to the south of the house.

OPPOSITE The white-flowered musk-scented flowers of 'Rambling Rector' rose make it a worthy incumbent of the 'ecclesiastical' border.

BELOW The strikingly scarlet Papaver orientale glows against the mute colours of the purple elder Sambucus nigra 'Guincho Purple'.

OPPOSITE The upright yews along the back of the house were planted about 100 years ago by a Yeatman-Biggs' ancestor who was a bishop. In front of the yews is a neatly shaped standard honeysuckle in a tub.

BELOW Domes of Hebe subalpina *and large clumps of* Iris sibirica *surround the pond and hold together the design of this secret garden.*

At the furthest corner of the garden is an ancient apple orchard where snowdrops and daffodils have naturalized. No one could remember the names of the apples, so Susannah employed a metal detector to find many of the original lead labels still buried in the soil beneath. They included such cultivars as 'Mr Prothero', a local speciality which is no longer available in cultivation. Susannah's father is a fruit farmer and arranged for all the trees to be budded and planted in a new young orchard at Long Hall. So it is not just four generations of Yeatman-Biggs who have loved and laboured for this dreamy Wiltshire garden, but their in-laws, too, who have been drawn into the task of preserving and enhancing its timeless beauty for generations to come.

Finlaystone

OPPOSITE The autumn colours of Peltiphyllum peltatum steal the show in the borders of the New Garden beneath the old laundry house.

BELOW Finlaystone is set in an extensive park, which matches the scale of the house and the Clyde Valley stretching away below.

The history of Finlaystone is as romantic as any. For four centuries it belonged to the Earls of Glencairn. Robert Burns stayed here under the patronage of the 14th (and last) Earl and wrote in 1791 ' I'll remember thee, Glencairn and a' that thou hast done for me!' But for over a century now it has belonged to George MacMillan, chief of Clan MacMillan, and his forebears.

The handsome stone house lies on the south side of the Clyde between Langbank and Port Glasgow, and it is set among sweeping lawns, with majestic views across the river. Its oldest links with its romantic past are a magnificent lime avenue that runs right down to the river, and an ancient yew tree under which John Knox is said to have held a communion of the Reformed Church in 1556. Subsequently, a later generation of occupants decided that Knox's yew tree was rather too close to the house because it took too much light from the window where the ladies of the family did their needlework: so it was moved to its present position at the edge of the parterre.

Much of the garden was laid out when the house was substantially enlarged in about 1900. The formal garden to the west of the house dates from this period and is enclosed within a yew hedge that was castellated by an enthusiastic family governess and a French aunt in about 1920. But it is George MacMillan, his wife

Jane, his sister Judy Hutton, and George MacMillan and Judy Hutton's mother, the late Lady MacMillan, who created the imaginative and beautiful garden seen today.

On the eastern side of the house, Lady MacMillan laid out the New Garden which, contrary to its name, dates from as long ago as 1959. It spreads across either side of a burn, which flows past the gabled stone building that once served the estate as a laundry. Several waterfalls intensify the romantic appeal of the New Garden, as do the weeping cherries hanging over the water's edge. The banks are lined with hostas, *Peltiphyllum peltatum* – spectacular in autumn – and azaleas, which blend into the woodland beyond. Indeed, throughout Finlaystone, the woodland areas are thick with azaleas, as well as rhododendrons, bluebells and snowdrops.

Celtic themes are one of the sources that have inspired the MacMillans to construct several new gardens on the hillside above the house. Jane MacMillan's Celtic Garden, for example, consists of an intricate pattern of paving set into grass: the design is based on one taken from the *Book of Kells*. Elsewhere, in the Walled Garden, there is a 'garden oasis' in the form of a Celtic cross with a pool at the centre. As a finishing touch, the cross and pool are enclosed by a circular brick rose pergola. Then, in 1986, Judy Hutton laid out a garden of scented plants for blind visitors, which is sometimes known as the Fragrant Garden, and on other occasions as the Smelly Garden.

George MacMillan was responsible for the splendid hexagonal folly that stands so invitingly on the edge of the top lawn. It makes great and excellent use of re-cycled materials: the folly's walls came from a recently demolished church in Port Glasgow and the rafters were re-used from old farm buildings. It typifies the inventiveness of this charming and romantic garden where Finlaystone's own romantic history has been enhanced by allusions to Scottish history and the whole wide world of the Celts.

LEFT A large and handsome head looks out from a bed of potentillas and ferns at the bottom of these steps, which lead down from the driveway.

OVERLEAF The castellated yew hedge that surrounds the spacious formal garden at Finlaystone dates back to c.1920.

Ninfa

Ninfa is a deserted medieval town in the Pontine marshes south of Rome. Spread among the ruins of its houses, churches, and fortifications, is the most beautiful and romantic garden in the world. The town was founded, flourished and died in the Middle Ages. At its greatest extension, it had one monastery and seven churches: Pope Alexander III was consecrated Pope in the largest church, Santa Maria Maggiore. In 1297, Boniface VIII bought Ninfa for his nephew Pietro Caetani. In 1382, however, the town was completely destroyed in one of the many civil wars that plagued the Papal states during the Avignon Captivity and the Great Schism. The sacking of Ninfa coincided with a period of economic contraction and the arrival of malaria in the Pontine marshes, leaving the town desolate, still a fief of the Caetani, but no more than a romantic ruin. Gregorovius called it the 'Pompeii of the Middle Ages'.

The English-born Duchess Ada Caetani began to clear the scrub from the ruins in about 1890 and planted many climbing roses against the newly-revealed walls. But today's garden has been created by her granddaughter Lelia, the last of the Caetani, and Lelia's English husband Hubert Howard. Throughout the 1950s and 1970s they intensified the plantings in quantity and variety. Eventually they set up a private Foundation, under their wills, to preserve the garden and castle in perpetuity.

The garden covers about 8 hectares (20 acres) and has an alkaline soil. A vast river flows out of the limestone rock immediately behind the old Caetani castle. The ubiquity of water allows plants to be irrigated during the dry months that would otherwise not survive the heat of an Italian summer. It also creates a cool freshness and a smell of growth that are unique to the garden: temperatures are often several degrees lower within the walls of Ninfa than outside.

OPPOSITE The castellated keep of the Caetani castle is seen here from across one of the leats which run through the garden.

BELOW The rock garden covers part of the town's ruined walls. San Biagio's ruined apse forms the backdrop.

PREVIOUS PAGE The wooden bridge in the middle of the garden is seen here with the castle and palace in the background.

OPPOSITE Every wall at Ninfa seems to be covered with rambling roses and other climbing plants. Flowering Judas trees are particularly magnificent in spring.

BELOW Despite the hot climate, there is constant flowing water at Ninfa which gives rise to luxurious growth in spring and summer.

The entrance drive leads along poplar-lined canals with a hedge of *Rosa roxburghii* on one side, past huge bushes of oleanders and overgrown box hedges as much as 8m (26ft) high. It then passes through an inner gate and into a courtyard that once formed the main square of the town, with the walls of the Caetani castle on one side and the Palazzo Comunale at the far end. The walls of the palazzo are festooned with white wisterias, the climbing rose 'Mermaid' with its great sulphur yellow single flowers, and red bougainvillaeas. A huge bush of the wintersweet *Chimonanthus praecox* flourishes against its western side, and other large specimens have been planted nearby to scent the air at Christmas time. The main river runs along the eastern side of the Palazzo Comunale and a dramatic staircase descends from the grand salone to a small sheltered area on the embankment. Here, underneath a pergola of honeysuckle, roses and *Clematis viticella* 'Purpurea Plena Elegans' are more sweet scented plants. Beyond a speeding mill race, a glade of magnolias is underplanted with spring bulbs.

Ninfa has been planted in the natural style, according to the English taste, and at no time has any attempt been made to Italianize the gardens: there are no straight lines, clipped hedges of box, yew trees shaped in cones, nor any statue, fountain, pool or stone ornament in any part. The ruins of the medieval town alone are enough to produce extraordinarily charming effects. Every wall and hummock seems to have a rose or other climbing plant draped over it: clematis, honeysuckle, passion flower, jasmine, wisteria, bignonia, and tecoma. One of the principal walks is along the banks of the river, which is spanned by several bridges. Stand on one of them and admire the vast clumps of the giant *Gunnera manicata*. The

cliffs of the hill town of Norma are seen beyond the limits of the town walls as a distant back drop, high in the sky.

Ninfa is quite unlike any other garden, for the intensely romantic setting of a deserted medieval town has no parallel. The lawns and woodlands appear so natural that it is difficult to realize that all the trees have been planted since 1920 and that Ninfa is an abandoned town invaded by a garden rather than a park containing ruins. It is often compared to English gardens – Sissinghurst, Nymans and Mount Usher, for example – but the disposition of plants around and over the ruined walls of a medieval town is unlike anything, anywhere else.

Moreover, Ninfa is a garden almost without structure. The main paths lead around the ruins, through gaps in walls, across yards and alleys, by bridges and gates that seem to bear little relation to the

medieval layout. It needs many hours of exploration to understand how the pieces fit together. The absence of plant labels adds to its Elysian quality, while the exclusion of statues and other artefacts is also an essential part of its character. There is a lost endeavour attached to vanished cities that inspires awe: Ninfa has some of the same spirit that pervades Mistra and Petra. The mystery of these abandoned towns excites the imagination, and the act of embellishing them with flowers transforms an archaeological relic into a place of rare enchantment.

ABOVE A pink American dogwood flowers against the background of the deeper pink Judas tree. Gunneras thrive at the edge of the river.

RIGHT The banks of the main river, seen from the edge of the town. The banks are planted with trees and shrubs that flower differently throughout the year.

Painter's Palette

Chilcombe is a tiny hamlet on a steep, south-facing hillside, sheltered from the north by beech trees and sycamores behind. It amounts to no more than a brace of cottages, John Hubbard's stone farmhouse, a farmyard and a tiny church embedded in its heart. John is an artist but perhaps he should have been a photographer: the strong lines and symmetries of his garden make it marvellously photogenic. It is, for the most part, a sequence of tightly enclosed, small rooms: the scale is intimate and cottagey. Indeed, it must be the most densely cultivated garden in the south of England.

John Hubbard's achievement has been to pile on the plants, layer after layer, season after season, to create strikingly different effects. Plants are chosen for their interesting forms, shapes and leaves and added to all the time, so that the garden continues to intensify. Few gardens show such profusion, make such good use of space, or double-up the planting on such an intensive scale. To prevent the scheme from becoming too disparate, all is held together by a strong evergreen structure and by repeating certain favourite plants throughout the garden to give it unity. Pulmonarias, pansies, *Viola cornuta* and foxgloves in apricot, white and purple are just a few of the plants that are used in this way.

ABOVE A welcome contrast lies beyond the busyness of the Walled Garden.

PREVIOUS PAGE The Kitchen Garden: nursery beds and herbaceous plants can be more evident than vegetables.

OPPOSITE Mediterranean-style, sun-loving plants like cistus, thyme and hyssop, surround a pot of marigolds.

The little courtyard in front of the house, cobbled and paved, is home to naturalized geraniums, campanulas, helianthemums, *Lychnis coronaria* and *Verbena bonariensis*. A Gothic archway leads out into a long lawn, which runs along the front of the house and is barely separated from the extensive paddock beyond. An effect of space is felt here as in no other part of the garden. Yet the walls offer shelter: late-flowering *Schizostylis coccinea*, *Salvia patens* and arum lilies *Zantedeschia aethiopica* enjoy their protection. Here, too, is an evergreen luxuriance of *Euphorbia characias*, plants of *Bupleurum fruticosum* 2m (6ft 6in) high, and ceanothus on the house itself.

The main garden lies below the house, a rough square on the south eastern slopes. It is walled on three sides and extends to about 0.6 hectare (1½ acres), divided into an endless number of small rectangular areas. At the bottom is a cow shed, now converted to changing rooms for the swimming pool which looks out over the South Dorset Downs to the hills behind the coastline. Low box hedges define the internal boundaries and give form to the structure. The lines of the design are firm, but often narrowed and hemmed in by the growth of plants, which makes views seem longer than they are. All the entrances and exits are flanked by architectural plants that emphasize the formal nature of the design: a pair of *Laurus nobilis* trimmed to 3m (10ft) cones marks the passage between the orchard and the kitchen garden. The gloriously classical plant *Acanthus spinosus* grows on either side of a gateway in the wall and a honeysuckle arbour dramatically emphasizes the junction of two paths.

The main entrance to the enclosed garden runs between two vast Irish yews and under a pergola hung with clematis, honeysuckles, jasmine, the early-flowering rambler rose 'Albéric Barbier' and the late-flowering favourite 'Blush Noisette'. An archway of the old *Rosa multiflora* rambler 'Goldfinch' connects the Herb Garden to the Sundial Garden, an area of sheltered open space and here the central path is lined with lavender and irises a-plenty. Both gardens are surrounded on two sides by dwarf apple trees trained as espaliers with such clematis as *C.* 'Etoile Violette' and *C. rehderana* growing up through them. The Herb Garden supports purple sage, rue and a profusion of tradescantias, sisyrinchiums, diascias and potentillas. A large

OPPOSITE This contrast of colours and shapes – tall, elegant pinks and mauves on one side, squat, compact yellows and creams on the other – typifies the intensive planting to be found at Chilcombe.

BELOW Sweet-scented Lilium regale blends its colours but contrasts its shape with nearby silver-leaved Stachys byzantina.

flowering cherry shelters a lichen-encrusted bench: salvias, penstemons and *Dorycnium hirsutum* surround it.

The Kitchen Garden proper occupies several intricately geometric beds at the bottom of the Walled Garden. Most of these are slightly raised, with box bobbles at the centre; some are edged with *Aster ericoides*. Here, too, are nursery beds where plants are grown on before being transplanted into the garden: cuttings, propagations and gifts from other gardeners. Gooseberries, trained as standards, march around two sides of the Kitchen Garden and define its boundaries.

It is not just the design and planting that make Chilcombe such a complex garden. John Hubbard is also a discriminating and adventurous plantsman. The top part of the walled garden has a central border where forms of *Salvia greggii* and *S. × jamensis* are grown as herbaceous plants: many come from the famous Compton-d'Arcy-Rix expeditions to Mexico. Here, too, are *Solanum jasminoides* 'Album' and *Akebia quinata*. On a hot bank, *Euphorbia mellifera*, *Pittosporum tenuifolium* and *Melianthus major* have been underplanted by artemisias and geraniums. A luxuriant specimen of *Rosa* 'Crimson Conquest' fills a south-facing wall at the highest corner of the walled garden. It has been layered and laid back against the wall so that it presents a density of flowers which, in an early season, will start at the beginning of May. Here and throughout the garden at Chilcombe, it is the catholicity of John Hubbard's tastes, the sheer variety of the plants and the scope of the plantsmanship that are so impressive.

ABOVE *The entrance to and exit from this classic double herbaceous border is marked by elegant young Irish yews rising above neatly clipped hedges.*

OPPOSITE *Large clumps of lavender thrive beneath this short pergola hung with* Rosa *'Goldfinch'.*

Sticky Wicket

No garden-owner has a finer sense of colour than Pam Lewis. Open any new book about the use of colour in the garden and you can be certain that Pam's garden at Sticky Wicket will be carefully described and illustrated by the most distinguished commentators. She is at the cutting edge of this most English of modern art forms.

When Pam and her husband bought Sticky Wicket in 1986, their principal concern was that their garden should blend with the surrounding countryside. 'We really do have to do something serious about this destruction of habitats', Pam asserts. 'Gardeners can do a little to regenerate pockets of it. And offer some sanctuary to the species which are fleeing the advance of modern farming.' This is precisely what the garden at Sticky Wicket aims to be: at one with nature.

The first parts of the garden to be developed were the Frog Garden and the Bird Garden near the house. Although made to attract wildlife, they were also planted with distinct colour schemes. The Frog Garden – best in spring and summer – brings together various shades of yellow, contrasting them with a range of blues; the Bird Garden experiments with pinks and purples.

Pam also loves the discipline and order of design, which she learnt from the example of John Brookes. She says that he made

ABOVE The slightly blue-ish pink of the classic climbing rose 'New Dawn' is perfectly picked up by the flowers of Fuchsia magellanica *'Sharpitor'.*

RIGHT This masterly grading of pinks and mauves is achieved by placing Achillea *'Cerise Queen' and sidalceas in front of stately* Filipendula rubra *'Venusta' and* Rosa *'Pink Perpétue' and carpeting the foreground with seedling violas.*

ABOVE *The spiky grey leaves of* Ononis spinosa *contrast with the purple mass of* Lavandula angustifolia *'Hidcote'.*

PREVIOUS PAGE Colours in the Round Garden are graded from strong purples in the centre to pale purples and creams in the foreground: they contrast with yellows in another section of the colour wheel behind.

her more analytical, better able to understand the structure of things. 'You can also play around with proportions, form and perspectives by considering the lines and distances between objects and plants – and of the design – and the variations between them', says Pam.

But it is to see her way with plants and colours that thousands flock to Sticky Wicket. Pam defines her garden as the place to study and demonstrate the art of planting, a place to experiment with associations of colour, form and texture of both foliage and flowers. Much of the enjoyment comes from the anticipation and the planning. Indeed, she works out many of her schemes by cutting flower pictures from seed catalogues and matching or contrasting them for colour. The printed colour may be an inaccurate guide to their colour in the garden, but the experiments with paper cut-outs serve to sharpen Pam's eye.

Pam studies the exact colours of plants with great care when composing her associations. She finds that yellows and pinks combine well if they are modified by paler shades like cream, which bind them together: they will co-exist provided no white or blue or mauve is added to destroy the harmony. One especially satisfying combination comes from using purple-leaved *Anthirrhinum majus* 'Black Prince', *Beta vulgaris* 'Bull's Blood' and *Atriplex hortensis* var. *rubra* as foils for the pink flowers of valerian *Centranthus ruber*, foxgloves *Digitalis* × *mertonensis* and *Diascia rigescens*.

It is in the Round Garden, with its three concentric gravel paths, that Pam's creative originality is most completely expressed. The boss at the centre is entirely planted with chamomile and shaped like an ancient earthwork with two bulwarks. It dominates the design: the garden as a whole occupies a long 0.8-hectare (2-acre) triangle, and the round garden fills much of the middle. This is the part of the garden, too, where scent matters the most, not just to give pleasure to the owners, but because fragrance always attracts numerous insects.

The Round Garden is a true colour wheel. It is intended to be enjoyed at its best in late summer. Not only do the shades flow through all the colours of the rainbow, but they are also arranged so that brighter colours are at the outside rim and they melt towards softer shades at the centre. Pam wants to convey the sense of being among the plants, absorbed by them and absorbing them in some mystical sense. She likens the gardener to an actor-manager, organizing a series of tableaux and performances. She believes that when people design or visit gardens they do not take sufficient account of the difference between those parts of the garden which are intended to be seen from a particular viewpoint and compose a picture in themselves, and those where the greatest aesthetic benefit comes from moving around inside it. The Round Garden is both the heart of the garden and its stillest point.

ABOVE In the background, Cornus controversa 'Variegata' is the perfect foil for stately upright grasses.

ABOVE *The flowers of pink scabious and purple* Lavandula angustifolia *'Hidcote' make a stimulating contrast of colour and shape.*

The newest part of Sticky Wicket is the White Garden, furthest away from the house at the top of the garden. It is the most informally planted part of the garden. White is the colour of hedgerows, and so – fitting in with the owner's garden beliefs – the white plantings assert its ecological credentials. Pam believes that such plantings pull the whole garden together. 'At the top I just want a nice fuzzy muddle', she says, 'eventually it will resemble thickets on a common and merge the garden with the natural world outside.'

ABOVE The glaucous seed heads of
opium poppies pick up the shapes of
crimson Allium sphaerocephalon *all of*
which are set off by the surrounding
pale pink flower heads.

LEFT Salvia sclarea *var.* turkestanica *is*
a very useful mixer because its flowers
and bracts contain so many shades of
pink, purple and cream.

Park Farm

Jill Cowley bought Park Farm, but not the land that went with it, in 1979. That was sold off separately. She acquired 0.8 hectare (2 acres), a pretty Elizabethan farmhouse, a dainty Gothic dairy (which has been converted for additional living space) and a splendid old barn that sheltered the house from traffic on the road. Unfortunately, the barn fell down on the day Jill signed the purchase contract, closing the road for two days and leaving mountains of bricks, tiles and timbers all over the front part of the garden.

Things could only get better. Jill had gardened before and knew what she wanted to do, which was to create as many habitats and as much shelter and variety as possible, while preserving the ravishing view across the River Chelmer to ancient parkland beyond. When she first moved in, there was nothing around the house except a stately walnut, planted in about 1930, a few neglected old apple trees and a venerable yew, which provided all the seedlings for the hedges she set about planting. Structure came first: the garden was split into many small sections, which have the paradoxical effect of making it seem much larger. Some of the materials were ready to hand: the paths are lined with the thousands of old bricks that littered the garden from the days when it had been a farmyard. Then Jill planted the trees that she particularly wanted to grow: they included *Acer davidii* and *Acer grosseri* var. *hersii* grown from seed sent by the Royal Horticultural Society from its garden at Wisley. Most of the trees have thrived in this comfortable: it is salutary to reflect that they are now so large and yet so young.

Jill is, above all, an unashamed and enthusiastic rosarian. She is certain that no other genus offers such a variety of forms, colours, scents and sizes, nor such long periods of bloom and garden interest. She likes to place vigorous modern roses at the backs of borders to provide colour right through to the end of

OVERLEAF Jill Cowley believes that roses offer better garden value than any other flower. This is the old pink Bourbon rose 'Blairii No 2'.

OPPOSITE On the edge of the drive, 'Buff Beauty' intertwines with a Portugal laurel above spikes of white Canterbury bells and drifts of Alchemilla mollis.

BELOW Lilium regale, silver artemisias and the white-flowered form of Lychnis coronaria in the White Garden in front of the Gothic dairy.

autumn: her favourites are the rich yellow 'Chinatown', pink 'Queen Elizabeth', elegant pale crimson 'Cerise Bouquet', and that most reliable of all roses, glorious, white 'Iceberg'.

The rubble from the collapsed barn remained a problem. No amount of hacking with a pick-axe could rid the area of hundreds of years' compacted hard core. The only possible solution was to use the fallen bricks and timbers to build raised beds and fill them with soil from other parts of the garden. This part is now known as the Hot Garden – so called because (entirely by accident, she says) Jill planted mainly red, orange and yellow plants there. A succession of strongly coloured herbaceous staples include purple fennel, euphorbias and yellow-leaved sedges. Seasonal effects come from such stunners as orange perennial wallflowers (*Erysimum* sp.), *Iris* 'Frosted Gold', and such poppies as *Papaver spicatum* (syn *P. heldreichii*). Among the best roses are 'Scharlachglut', a brilliant clear red in high summer, and 'Graham Thomas', which produces its glorious golden globes late into the autumn. 'Climbing Lady Hillingdon' looks exquisite in front of the evergreen *Bupleurum fruticosum* and arches up into a yellow elder, *Sambucus nigra* 'Aurea' behind. On the edge of the drive, 'Buff Beauty' reaches up into a Portugal laurel. Other background plants – all of them evergreen – include the long-needled *Pinus wallichiana* and *Ilex aquifolium* 'Myrtifolia Aurea Maculata'.

The White Garden is particularly successful at Park Farm. The fine silvery *Salix exigua* – such a good plant but still little known – stands out against the yew hedge and Jill has underplanted it with *Campanula alliariifolia*, 'Iceberg' roses, white geraniums, and *Viburnum plicatum* 'Lanarth'. The huge white tree-poppies of *Romneya coulteri* billow around the seats. Behind

OPPOSITE A fastigiate juniper surrounded by Allium aflatunense *and columbines exemplifies Jill Cowley's sympathetic use of space and colour in her garden.*

BELOW Clematis florida *'Sieboldii' and a strikingly large-flowered form of* Jasminum officinale *flower together in the middle of summer.*

the hedge, there is more silver foliage, glistening on trees of *Salix alba* var. *sericea* and a white poplar.

The interesting thing about Jill Cowley's garden is that she is never satisfied with it. That is, of course, normal for any keen gardener, but in her case she says that the problem is that she herself has changed over the years. Her interests have moved on from those early days. She is a different person, and her enthusiasms are different too. She no longer plants her gardens according to colour schemes, but takes some other unifying theme as her starting point. The stately walnut close to the kitchen door, for example, stretches out its protective branches to fill a large courtyard. Here is the Winter Garden, planted partly with such evergreens as *Mahonia bealei*, *Itea ilicifolia* and *Sarcococca hookeriana* whose white, sweet-scented flowers appear at the same time as last year's shiny black berries. The underplantings include Mr Bowles's golden grass *Millium effusum* 'Aureum', masses of snowdrops, aconites and hellebores and rows of orange-fruited *Iris foetidissima*. Classical statues fill the corners, including a handsome likeness of Caesar Augustus as a young man. Here, too, is a single spring-flowering shrub which lends its name to the whole garden: *Viburnum* 'Park Farm', named in 1924, long before Jill was even born.

The Chinese Garden, inspired by a visit to Suchow, is also planted thematically, primed by plants that Jill brought back from her trip. A *Paulownia* tree – not entirely happy in the cold winds of Essex – was grown from seed collected in the Imperial Palace in Peking. Here, too, are two Chinese nameless roses grown from cuttings which Jill describes as 'repeat-flowering forms of *chinensis* with a bit of *Rosa multiflora* in them – quite like 'Trier'.' The beautiful *Pinus bungeana* is here: so are the sacred *Nandina domestica*, *Ligustrum quihoui* and *L. lucidum*, Chinese paeonies, lilies, *Rosa willmottiae* and any amount of paving, gravel, pots, materials and artefacts which recall China.

No account of Park Farm can fail to mention the importance of Jill's elderly donkey Benjamin. He is her companion, waste recycler and also her garden mulcher: his contribution to the garden's welfare is immense and cannot be understated.

LEFT Box hedges, lines of blue forget-me-nots and topiary yews frame a view out across the Chelmer Valley towards unspoilt ancient parkland.

THE GLORY OF ROSES

Helmingham Hall

A visit to Helmingham is a step back into history, to a time of ancient certainties, order and peace. The house is a moated manor, half-timbered when begun in 1480, but smartened up by a cladding of bricks and tiles in the 18th century. It is set in the most spacious imaginable 162-hectare (400-acre) deer-park, loosely studded with vast centennial oaks grown to their full spread.

The Tollemaches have lived here since 1487. There is no better place in which to study the cultivation of old garden roses.

Helmingham's formal garden lies beyond the moat to the south of the house. It is surrounded on three sides by a substantial rose garden begun in 1965 by the mother of the present Lord Tollemache. Some sixty hybrid musks, lightly pruned and allowed to billow out, fill the beds. They constitute a near-complete collection of musk roses, including such rarities as 'Daybreak', 'Thisbe' and 'Danaë', as well as the better-known 'Cornelia', 'Wilhelm', 'Vanity',

ABOVE The old striped gallica rose 'Rosa Mundi' was first recorded about the time that Helmingham Hall was finished in the 16th century.

LEFT Old rambler roses 'D. Perkins' run along the back of the borders in the walled garden, with Hollyhock *'Nigra' and* Achillea *'Cloth of Gold' in front.*

PREVIOUS PAGE The new rose garden around a statue of Flora is reached through a knot garden and beds of 'Rosa Mundi'.

ABOVE The formal garden in front of the wrought iron entrance gates to the walled garden is surrounded by a large planting of hybrid musk roses.

'Felicia' and 'Penelope'. The entire garden, which is about 100m (110yd) long, is edged with Hidcote lavender, underplanted with variegated London Pride, and complemented by *Campanula lactiflora*, alstroemerias, foxgloves and paeonies. This is gardening on a large scale, and makes its impact through simplicity and repetition: it is immensely grand.

Beyond the formal garden is the walled garden proper, built of brick in 1745. On either side of the central grassy path runs a broad and stately double herbaceous border, which is 110m (120yd) long. Climbing roses are tied to straining wires all along its back. The roses include 'Guinée', 'Long John Silver', *Rosa multiflora* var. *cathayensis*, 'John Hopper', 'Gruss an Teplitz', 'Climbing Richmond', 'Debutante', 'Mme Isaac Pereire', 'Adélaïde d'Orléans', 'Albertine', 'Ayrshire Queen', and several other Ayrshire roses that have been grown here for many years (and perpetuated by taking cuttings) but whose names are long since forgotten. All are rigorously thinned down to three or four new stems, cut back and tied in to cover the straining wires, but no more than that. The herbaceous plantings are chosen to blend with the soft colours of the roses: pinks, blues, mauves, whites and the palest of creamy-yellows show off the roses at high summer. Not until the main rose-flowering has finished in mid-August do yellows, bronzes, oranges and reds come to the fore.

A spring border runs all the way along one of the outer walls of the walled garden and is planted mainly with irises, tulips and paeonies. Against the wall are such fine roses as 'Gloire de Dijon', 'Sophie's Perpetual', 'Desprez à Fleurs Jaune', 'Seagull', 'Captain Hayward', 'Goldfinch' and 'Kitchener of Khartoum', as well as various and colourful vines, clematis, chaenomeles, ceanothus, and myrtle from Queen Victoria's wedding posy.

ABOVE Musk roses and lavender frame this entrance to the walled garden and its long herbaceous borders.

When the present Lady Tollemache came to Helmingham in 1975, she built on what she inherited from her mother-in-law and intensified what was already there. But she also made an entirely new formal rose garden on the eastern side of the moat. She wanted it to look as original as possible and harmonize not only with the existing garden but

also with the house and the deer park beyond. So well has this been achieved that already the knot gardens and yew hedges (planted in 1982) seem mature: the garden, planted with the help of Lady Salisbury, could have been here for hundreds of years. The knots include the Tollemaches' heraldic device, a fret or interlacing pattern of bands, which has been made to interweave by pruning the strips of box at different levels.

The rose garden leads into a herb garden and two beds of 'Rosa Mundi' (*Rosa gallica* 'Versicolor') are interplanted with 'The Fairy'. A statue of Flora garlanded with sandstone roses stands at the centre of a splendid collection of old-fashioned roses. Separate beds hold the albas and species roses, a selection of centifolias and mosses, a large choice of gallicas and so on. The selection is not limited to those that were known at some historical cut-off date. Likewise, the underplantings are of spring bulbs, white foxgloves, *Campanula persicifolia*, *Alchemilla mollis*, purple violas and various geraniums. One reason why the garden is so successful is that the roses and their companion plantings all fall within a narrow colour range: it is a discipline from which every rose-lover can learn.

One of the most remarkable and original features of the new garden is the way that some of the roses are tied down and pegged to wire hoops in the shape of a crinoline, standing 1.5m (6ft) high and wide. The roses break from every axil and produce a sheet of bloom. This technique of cultivation is Lady Tollemache's own invention, and the effect has been so consistently admired by visitors that now she makes the wire frames for sale.

Throughout the garden at Helmingham, the roses are given individual, loving attention. They are actively cultivated to an exceptionally high standard by the three professional gardeners who have spent their working lives in private service on this large estate. Furthermore, the triumph of human intervention over the vagaries of nature is seen not just among the roses but also in the immaculately edged lawns and the weedless borders. Everywhere at Helmingham, order prevails over anarchy. It is a fine achievement.

LEFT The crimson 'Wilhelm' and other hybrid musks are set off by campanulas and a long hedge of lavender at the front of the bed.

Wartnaby

Lady King has made Wartnaby one of the best modern examples of how to grow roses in mixed borders and it is well worth a visit. Here is the garden of a plantswoman who understands the importance of good design and the need to group plants for effect. Moreover, it is the garden of someone who likes roses and is prepared to make them one of the principal elements of the design; when the roses are not in flower, foliage shapes, colours and textures take over.

The house is modern, but built in the Jacobean style, and enjoys fine views of the English midlands. It is anchored in its garden by a broad terrace and a wide lawn which ends in a ha-ha, that wonderful 18th-century device for bringing the landscape closer to the house. A border runs along the edge of the lawn, just below the terrace, and it is no secret that this border has been getting wider in recent years as yet more lawn is turned over and planted – always a sign of a garden in the ascendant. Here, the wonderfully scented and reliable Portland rose 'Jacques Cartier' grows here, surrounded by *Geranium pratense* 'Albiflorum' and hardy pinks, backed by the white poppies and blue-grey leaves of *Romneya coulteri*: there is no doubt that Lady King knows how to plant her roses to

ABOVE Dianthus *'Lady Constance Finnis' is the perfect foil for* Rosa *'Constance Spry' growing voluptuously overhead.*

LEFT Roses and herbaceous plants combine beautifully as they are all in the pink-purple colour range.

best effect, with generous mixed plantings with ornamental shrubs and herbaceous plants.

This is particularly apparent in the formal rose-garden, a split-level enclosure with a small, oval lily-pond in the lower part. Even here, roses do not dominate. Instead, they are interplanted with other shrubs, like ceanothus, hebes and tree paeonies (*P. lutea* var. *ludlowii*) and underplanted with geraniums. Narcissus and muscari provide colour in spring. The collection of roses is a good one: 'Variegata di Bologna', 'Camaieux' and 'Jeanne de Montfort' are names which indicate that Lady King knows her cultivars and chooses the best. To ensure a maximum number of varieties, only one specimen of each has been planted: they are held together by herbaceous plantings and the firm design. Vigorous roses are tied into a wooden framework, so that their over-floppy wands can be kept firmly under control.

About half of the roses are repeat-flowerers, which means that the garden has roses from early summer to late autumn. Blue agapanthus associate wonderfully with the creamy-yellow noisette 'Céline Forestier'; geraniums and sedums surround 'Ferdinand Pichard', picking up the crimsons and pinks of its stripy flowers. Modern hybrids like David Austin's English rose 'William Shakespeare' associate well with genuinely ancient cultivars; 'Gertrude Jekyll' looks positively radiant between the old Bourbon 'La Reine Victoria' and the even older moss rose 'Blanche Moreau'.

Off to one side is the white garden, where there are four box-edged beds of the old polyantha rose 'Yvonne Rabier', and white 'Mrs Sinkins' pinks, and white-flowered annuals occupy the centre of the quincunx. All around the outside are roses in mixed plantings: the old gallica 'Blanchefleur' keeps company with *Hebe albicans*, *Iris foetidissima* 'Variegata', white foxgloves and a white form of *Viola cornuta* in front. There are lessons in good planting, too, in the adjoining purple-pink border. The old mauve gallica rose 'Président de Sèze' is next to the violet-blue *Buddleja davidii* 'Black Knight' in a grouping that includes *Heuchera* 'Palace Purple', the purple *Euphorbia amygdaloides* 'Purpurea', *Penstemon* 'Garnet' and *Rosa glauca* itself. Nearby, the

RIGHT A section of the border rose-filled border underplanted with varied shrubs and herbaceous plants. The border is also featured on the previous page.

great purple moss rose 'William Lobb' is underplanted by *Ophiopogon planiscapus* 'Nigrescens', dicentras and the purple weigela.

The substantial kitchen garden and orchard are formally laid out and entirely enclosed by hedges of *Cupressocyparis leylandii* that are 5m (16ft) high. The firm design and decorative planting make it possible to screen the working parts of the kitchen garden from the ornamental. The long central path is flanked by massed plantings of hybrid musks, including 'Felicia' and 'Pink Prosperity', underplanted with the grey-leaved *Stachys byzantina* and *Lychnis flos-jovis*, and edged with lavender and box. Arches have been planted with ramblers like 'Aimée Vibert' and 'Sander's White Rambler', complemented by such clematis as 'Mme Julia Correvon' and 'Proteus' to extend the flowering season.

The photographs on these pages were taken before Lady King undertook her latest reorganization of the garden. This involved strengthening the design of the sunken rose garden, taking out the Italian cypresses, planting and replanting many new rose cultivars, separating the colours, and putting one area entirely to herbaceous plants. Work continues: the new arboretum is already making a fine show; a new herb garden has just been planted. Indeed, scarcely a season passes without a substantial new project being undertaken.

OPPOSITE A view through the rose garden: the cypresses have since been removed to restore the sense of scale.

BELOW The modern classic 'Iceberg', underplanted here with purple sage and lavender.

Elsing Hall

David and Shirley Cargill bought Elsing Hall in 1984. The house (flint-faced, with stone quoins) dates back to 1470 but was thoroughly Gothicized by the Victorians: its spooky outline would pass as a black-and-white illustration from Edgar Allan Poe. Giant hogweeds seed around the front door, their outsize stateliness quite appropriate to the scale of the gabled hall. Overwhelmed by the romantic beauty of its rose-clad chimneys and the exuberant growth of the climbing roses which enfold its walls, a visitor called Elsing the Sleeping Beauty Garden. There is no better place to enjoy the wild romantic way of growing roses.

Back in 1984, there was no garden to speak of. The grounds were derelict, the walled garden impenetrable: the only possible strategy was slash and burn. The Cargills decided to tackle the terracing in front of the house first. Here they planted a fascinating mixture of roses: 'Centenaire de Lourdes' (a great favourite in France, but all too seldom seen in England), the lanky purple 'William Lobb', pink 'Fimbriata' whose petals are fringed like a carnation, the sumptuous mauve-pink 'Ardoisée de Lyon', and dainty white 'Katharina Zeimet'. These five roses represent five different classes of rose and are, respectively, a shrub rose, a moss, a *rugosa* hybrid, a hybrid perpetual and a polyantha rose. The Cargills' taste in roses is both catholic and voracious.

Against the walls of the house are the opulent climber with pink wavy petals 'Mme Grégoire Staechelin', the exquisite pearl-pink 'Mme Alfred Carrière' and that classic with a modern look 'Fantin Latour',

ABOVE Huge plants of the giant hogweed Heracleum mantegazzianum *line the drive across the moat that runs around Elsing Hall.*

OPPOSITE 'Impératrice Joséphine' is the best of the little-known 'Frankfurt' roses. Its soft petals flourish in the dry air of eastern England.

ABOVE A relaxed profusion of shrubs and climbing roses such as 'William Lobb' (left) and 'Centenaire de Lourdes' (right) fills the terrace on the south side of the house. Rose 'Albertine' grows against the house.

normally a shrub but here 4m (13ft) high. Vigorous groundcover plants underscore the roses and spread themselves around: seedlings and foundlings of fennel, hellebores and geranium are welcome, even in cracks between the paving. The huge grey thistle *Onopordon arabicum* self-seeds in the lawn below and is spared by the mower.

The Cargills are enthusiastic plantsmen: their garden is a celebration of the sheer variety of the plant kingdom. They already grow more than 400 different roses, and the number rises annually. They have a relaxed approach to the demands of maintenance: besides, most roses flourish on benign neglect. They go on flowering year after year with little or no attention. There are better ways of passing time as a gardener than following the conventional routines of spraying, pruning and training – planting more roses, for instance. The Cargills understand how to obtain the maximum return from a minimum investment. This is liberation gardening.

The benefit of this attitude can be seen when the lawn in front of the house is covered in fritillaries in April and marsh orchids in June. It can be seen, too, in the way the climbing roses are allowed to flop right down to the edge of the moat. Old white ramblers are among the most effective, a tumult of bloom in high summer when reflected in the water, especially the vast *multiflora* rambler 'White Flight', the most sumptuous and generous of the small-flowered white ramblers 'Bobbie James', and the famous evergreen hybrid 'Félicité et Perpétue'.

The door into the walled garden is hung with a vast mass of the late-flowering rambler 'Wedding Day'. The south-facing walls are planted with climbing and rambling roses, which the Cargills have allowed to tumble forward across the shrub roses in front, rather than spending weeks and months tying them in. The protection of the wall encourages roses to grow to unusual heights. The rich purple shrub rose 'Zigeunerknabe' grows to about 2.5m (8ft), while the shapely pink damask 'Marie Louise' (named after the Emperor Napoleon's second wife) has reached to the top of the 3m (10ft) wall and David Austin's modern classic, the myrrh-scented 'Constance Spry', has climbed up to 6m (20ft).

This garden is kept grassed over and hundreds of roses are grown in circles cut out of the turf. The old fruit trees, which the Cargills rescued from near-terminal neglect – apples, plums and a medlar – have climbers growing up them, clematis and honeysuckle as well as roses. Here are the oldest English

BELOW A Gothic archway frames this view of the plantings around the house. The cream rose 'Dunwichensis' grows at the edge of the gravel.

rambler rose 'The Garland', bred by Wells in the early 1830s, and the vigorous climbing form of the elegantly scrolled 'Mlle Cécile Brunner' growing alongside such imposing clematis as the double-flowered *C. viticella* 'Alba Luxurians'. Sometimes roses and other climbers have been planted together. The deep yellow climbing rose 'Lawrence Johnston' flowers only once – prolifically – in May: the Cargills have sent it up the same tree as *Clematis fargesii*, which produces its satiny white flowers continuously from June to September.

On the edge of the moat is a copse of semi-wild roses, planted for shelter, a screen from the south-west wind. Here are the creamy-white semi-double shrub 'Frühlingsanfang', one of Lord Penzance hybrid briars 'Anne of Geierstein', and 'Ruga', an old cross between *Rosa gallica* and Shakespeare's musk rose, the British native *Rosa arvensis*. But Elsing is much more than a rose garden. Alongside the moat also are bamboos, *Caltha polypetala*, a patch of *Matteuccia struthopsis* under a huge weeping ash, skunk cabbages, *Ligularia dentata* 'Desdemona', *Gunnera manicata* and *G. tinctoria*: all are vigorous plants, lush growers, nudging each other for space.

The Cargills are keen on modern sculpture: they point out that it costs half the price of 18th-century pieces but does not get stolen. They are also enthusiastic re-users of architectural salvage within their garden. For example, an avenue of ginkgos leads from a pretty pavilion to a stone archway that was rescued from the Corn Hall in Peterborough. Likewise, the steeple garden is dominated by a slate-hung chimney stack with a tall finial: the 16 square beds around it each have Irish yews trained to match the shape of the chimney, a reminder that David and Shirley Cargill are just as much at ease with formal gardens as informal.

OPPOSITE Sir Frederick Stern's popular climbing rose 'Wedding Day', interplanted with honeysuckle, luxuriously clothes the entrance to the walled garden.

BELOW A large plant of 'The Garland', the oldest climbing rose that has been bred in England.

GARDENING IN A
DRY CLIMATE

Cetinale

There are three gardens at Cetinale: the 19th-century Italian garden at the entrance; the 20th-century flower garden beneath the ramparts, and the grand baroque garden made by Carlo Fontana for Cardinal Fabio Chigi of Siena, which runs up to the Romitorio at the top of the hill behind. That any of them survives is due to the work of Lord Lambton, who bought the estate in 1977 and the Romitorio in 1990.

The old approach to Cetinale was originally by a long avenue of clipped ilexes at the end of which Cardinal Chigi placed a massive statue of Hercules. Nowadays, however it is reached along a dusty road and through the yard of the farm belonging to the estate. The formal garden in front of the house is prettily laid out with box hedges, grass-filled parterres, clipped yew topiaries and lemon-trees in pots: all very Tuscan, but, in fact, late 19th-century Italianate. There are lemon trees in new terracotta pots at the corners, and allegorical statues that have been carved to represent Abundance by one of the Mazzuoli. The main axis of the garden is quite extraordinary as it runs right through the ground floor of the house, and out again in a long broad avenue on the other side: 'an unusually protracted vista' the American Rose Nicholls called it in 1929.

PREVIOUS PAGE The main approach to Cetinale leads through a formal 19th-century Italianate garden to arrive at the front door.

OPPOSITE Carlo Fontana's Romitorio that crowns the hill rising to the west of Cetinale.

There is an apt inscription over the porch at the villa of Cetinale which has been there since at least 1802 when James Forsyth noted it. Its translation is given overleaf.

ABOVE The formal gardens are decked out with lemon trees in traditional Tuscan terracotta pots.

*ABOVE Carlo Fontana built the chapel
at the side of the formal garden.*

Whoever you are who approach
That which may seem horrible to you
Is pleasing to myself.
If it appeals to you, remain.
If it bores you, go away.
Each is equally agreeable to me.

Lord Lambton has planted the walls of the villa and the olive orchards above it with such ornamental climbers as *Rosa* 'Mermaid', the climbing potato *Solanum crispum* and the blue flowers of *Clematis × jackmannii*. This modern overlay is a by-product of replanting the English Garden underneath the ramparts on the southern side. The garden is a series of smallish outdoor rooms that are connected by gravel paths and often symmetrically planted. A piece of grass, almost a lawn, at the edge of the swimming pool has two large bushes of wintersweet *Chimonanthus praecox* in the middle, while the borders around it are planted as matching images across a central axis.

Further down, a line of four secret gardens is traversed by a central gravel path. These miniature, mid-20th-century school-of-Sissinghurst rooms, the purest example of the style in Italy, form the most interesting part of the English Garden. Two of the secret gardens are devoted to the cultivation of vegetables, with the little pink polyantha rose 'The Fairy' all along the front. The other two gardens are kept purely for flowers, and among the roses are old-fashioned *Rosa gallica* 'Cardinal de Richelieu', the modern shrub 'Raubritter', and the cabbage rose *Rosa × centifolia*.

The secret gardens are separated by pergolas: one is covered with vines and underplanted with pale roses and Florentine irises, while another is wrapped in pink and white *Rosa wichurana* ramblers. Roses are not the only shrubs: a rich tangle of lilacs, hibiscus, deutzias and phlomis is underplanted with columbines, pansies, lavender, paeonies and lilies. The colour schemes here are English and cottagey: the soft pinks and purples of old-fashioned roses contrast with the harsh red of 'Scharlachglut' and the bright orange of the day lilies. The English Garden at Cetinale was not, as has sometimes been said, created by Lord Lambton and Claire Wood. The precise lines of the garden were laid down by either English

BELOW The clock tower in the olive orchards to the side of the house at Cetinale. A large pink pelargonium marks the top of a flight of stairs in the foreground.

or Scotch women who married Chigi marquesses in the early 19th and 20th centuries. No alteration whatsoever has been made to the plans and the nine yew and three cut box bushes in the kitchen and front gardens were planted at the beginning of the century.

A pair of loquats *Eriobotrya japonica* flanks the path that leads out of the secret gardens, through a cottage gate, and on to a walk lined with upright rosemary to a sequence of more open enclosures. A rough croquet lawn is fringed with almond trees and olives. An orchard of fruit trees, with everything from medlars to quinces, has climbing and trailing roses set to ramble up the old fruit trees in the conventional English manner. More roses and occasional shrubs, such as the purple form of smoke bush *Cotinus coggygria* 'Purpureus' are dotted around the mown grass. To one side is an avenue of young lime trees, which will develop as a feature of the garden in the future, while the retaining walls are covered with wild snapdragons, valerian and capers.

Fontana enlarged the house and laid out the garden for Cardinal Chigi, the nephew of Pope Alexander VII in the 1670s. A broad walled grass walk runs from the back of the villa to two brick gate piers decorated with copies of figures from Trajan's column in Rome. The walk then continues to the theatre, a natural amphitheatre at the foot of the Romitorio hill. Here begins the 240-step ascent to the hermitage at the top. The steps up to the hermitage form a sacred staircase. The woodland walks are lined with votive chapels and statues of penitents as an aid to meditation and prayer. Edward Hutton described Cetinale in 1955, after more than 50 years' acquaintance, and concluded: 'the most splendid thing here is the park called *La Tebaide*, to which a long grass path, wide as the house, between high walls, leads to another statued gateway with ivy-clad niches and obelisks and balls. Thence one passes into great *boschi* of ilexes, and thence by a rude flight of steps to Fontana's Romitorio on the highest point hereabout, to be rewarded by a wide and magnificent panorama all over the Sienese *contado*.' Little did Edward Hutton suspect that this prospect would soon be uncovered from the Tuscan wilderness and subsequently saved from decay by an English lord.

LEFT The English Garden beneath the house is informally planted with old-fashioned roses and herbaceous plants.

Beebe Yudell Garden

Buzz Yudell is an architect; Tina Beebe works as a colourist and garden designer. They bought their Malibu plot in 1982, started building in 1987 and moved in a year later: so the entire garden has been laid out and planted since then. The plot was long and narrow – 180m (600ft) long but only 30m (100ft) wide – and Buzz and Tina chose it partly for the splendid views of the ocean. But of more importance was the good soil (it had long been cultivated as a tomato farm) and the site was not too precipitous. At the top of the garden is a small citrus orchard with a wide choice of different fruits: citrus are hard work, even in this climate, but Buzz and Tina enjoy the reward of growing and eating their

ABOVE The steps down 'the street' are lined with pots of drought-tolerant aloes. Note how the garden beyond the pool merges with the native chaparral.

LEFT The Beebe-Yudell house was inspired by classical Italian forms. The lawns around the swimming pool are one of the few parts of the garden which are regularly irrigated.

ABOVE A grape-vine encloses this view from one of the garden rooms up to a pergola where 'Mme Alfred Carrière' frames the vista up an avenue of edible Feijoa sellowiana *fruit trees.*

OPPOSITE The early-flowering climbing rose 'Belle Portugaise' forms a ceiling for one of the outside 'rooms' opposite the main rooms of the house.

own produce. Right at the furthest end of the property is an olive orchard, merging into the natural vegetation beyond. These utilitarian plantings are a constant reminder of the garden's origin as a smallholding.

Buzz's house has echoes of Italian farmhouses: a modern re-interpretation of classical rural shapes. They decided to match it room for room by creating a series of garden rooms opposite the house, all the way down its side, and to pave the surface between the two: they now call this main axis 'the street'. The garden runs from north to south, and slopes a little as it goes. Buzz took advantage of this to create a stunning series of levels and steps along 'the street'. The drop in height is not significant, but enough to create a sense of movement, and it enables the swimming pool (at the bottom) to reflect the architecture of the house and the elegant staircases lined with pots.

The lawn around the swimming pool at the bottom is irrigated, but elsewhere the garden is more at one with nature. The pots that line the principal staircase have to be watered by hand, but the task is not laborious because they are planted with succulents like kniphofias and aloes, which thrive on little water and irregular watering. Water is expensive, so Tina has planted the garden in such a way that drought-tolerant shrubs take over as you move further away from the house towards the long western boundary. Here the garden merges into the native evergreens of the chaparral – magnificent ceanothus, bright yellow fremontodendrons, splendid toyons (*Heteromeles arbutifolia*) and spectacular Californian tree poppies *Romneya coulteri* which grow as much as 3m (10ft) high.

Tina is an enthusiastic rosarian. The old white noisette rose 'Mmè Alfred Carriere' is never out of flower where it rambles over the upper pergola. Opposite the house, trained on a frame as a ceiling for one of the garden rooms, is a fine specimen of the exquisite early-flowering

Rosa gigantea hybrid 'Belle Portugaise', a pink climber that has achieved much greater popularity on the coast of California than in its native Portugal. A special bed is devoted to David Austin's hybrids, where 'Proud Titania' grows as high as 4.25m (14ft), three times the size it attains in its native England. One of Tina's favourite David Austin roses is the pink 'Belle Storey' whose incurved petals remind her of the paeonies which – alas – she cannot grow in the climate of the Californian coast.

Tina is especially interested in colour. Indeed, she advises professionally on the colours of buildings. As a result, her garden contains some extremely interesting experiments with colour combinations. Evergreen euphorbias and the grey-yellow *Helichrysum petiolare* 'Limelight' are planted in front of the mahogany-barked *Arbutus marina*, while seasonal additions to the scheme comes from dark purple irises and the exquisite yellow-flowered *Crocosmia crocosmiiflora* 'Solfaterre' whose bronzy leaves bridge the spectrum. Annuals and bulbs then add more ephemeral colour. The native *Eschscholtzia californica* in its many shades and forms has seeded in every crack in the paving – so too, surprisingly, have alpine strawberries. South African bulbs are a great source of colour, throughout the garden, especially in winter and spring. The dainty iridaceous flowers of red *Lapeirousia laxa* (syn. *Anomatheca laxa*) are a great joy in spring, and there are babianas throughout the garden in every imaginable shade. Seldom does a garden show such vivid and determined use of colour, and yet blend so well with the wild vegetation of its setting.

ABOVE The paving in the upper part of 'the street' has been loosely laid in gravel, to encourage ephemeral annuals like the orange Californian poppy Eschscholtzia californica *to seed around. The building up behind is Tina's and Buzz's studio.*

OPPOSITE Close to the house, pots, roses, irises and bright annuals create an effect in early spring which is both architectural and colourful. The rose against the house is 'Climbing Mrs Sam McGredy'.

La Casella

La Casella was built near Grasse in the Alpes-Maritimes in 1960 as a copy of the neo-classical Hermitage de Pompadour at Fontainebleau and bought in 1983 by Tom Parr, chairman of the celebrated interior decoration company Colefax & Fowler, and Claus Scheinert. Parr has poured all the creativity and sensibility for which he is so well known into arranging and decorating the villa and its satellite buildings.

Apart from moving the swimming pool further down the hillside, so that the area immediately around the villa could be properly integrated into the interior arrangements, the present garden did not begin to take shape until Claus Scheinert got to work on it in 1984. Various garden experts had been wheeled in before that time to give the benefit of their advice, but most were English and few made any concessions to the hot, dry Mediterranean climate. By the end of their first season, all the plants they recommended had died. Scheinert himself had no experience of garden-making: indeed, he had never even owned a garden of his own. But he set himself to solve the problem with all the thoroughness of a native German and read avidly about the essentials for making a good garden in the south of France. He also visited all the famous old gardens of the Riviera, most notably Villa Noailles near Grasse, La Chèvre d'Or at Biot, and the Villa Hanbury at La Mortola, just across the frontier into Italy. Not only were these gardens an inspiration to Scheinert, but their owners proved to be founts of encouragement: often, too, their gardeners were generous sources of plants and practical advice.

So Claus Scheinert tackled the first of the eight steep olive terraces which now add up to La Casella's 1.5-hectare (3¾-acre) garden. Tom Parr laid down only one condition: that there should be no red flowers. Scheinert took the principle a stage further, and decided to limit his plantings to comparatively few species – no more than thirty – which

ABOVE La Casella is planted entirely with soft colours, among which blues and mauves predominate.

OPPOSITE The owners have gone to great lengths to create lawns of a lushness which set off the structure of the garden to perfection.

are repeated throughout the garden and thus help to unify its design. The rose garden, for example, is planted only with roses in pink and white. But all the plants are locally grown and chosen to survive months of neglect in a Mediterranean summer.

The first terrace he redesigned and planted is now known as the Myrtle Walk, because it is both edged with myrtle hedging and lined with individual myrtle plants in pots. The use of topiary in the French classical tradition was inspired by La Chèvre d'Or. The top terrace is laid out as a pergola whose pillars are made of rounded bricks. There are echoes of La Mortola in the gentle steps and stairways that run between the terraces. At the bottom is a citrus grove where the trees have been planted in individual squares of box and mulched with gravel.

PREVIOUS PAGE Water-loving arum lilies and Iris ochroleuca *in the pool contrast with wild acanthus growing in the foreground.*

Throughout the garden, the surfaces are infinitely variable: paths and terraces have been made of everything from brick and stone to rounded cobbles and gravels of different sizes and colours. On every level, the structure comes from evergreen plants and hedges, especially Italian cypresses *Cupressus sempervirens* 'Stricta'. Much of the background planting is supplied by lavender cotton (*Santolina*), rosemary, lavender, *Acanthus mollis*, box and jasmine, all of them evergreen natives, but differing enormously in the colour and texture of the leaves. The flowering plants are all in the pale pastel ranges: plumbago, echiums, romneyas, agapanthus and irises feature strongly.

Green colours dominate in winter. This is the time when the lawns, too, are seen at their best. Incredible though it sounds, at the beginning of the 19th century, the first fashionable settlers on the Riviera were in the habit of importing fresh turf by boat from England, and replacing

ABOVE White wisteria flowers spectacularly in the south of France, relishing the hot summers which encourage bud initiation.

OPPOSITE The sky-blue flowers of Plumbago capensis *tumble from an urn, in contrast with the tight formality of the topiary box spheres that grow below.*

OPPOSITE The blue flowers of a large species of agapanthus are massed here like bluebells in a formal garden.

BELOW A dark-flowered form of lavender makes a handsome scented hedge beneath the dark-leaved evergreen oaks.

it every year. Scheinert has gone to remarkable lengths to create lawns of astonishing lushness. Grass provides the perfect setting for all the structural parts of the garden. It is the lawns that also receive the lion's share of garden maintenance. They are aerated with a spiked roller in May and September and the holes that result from this treatment are then brushed full of fine silicate sand. The grass is fed regularly every six weeks, treated with a fungicide whenever necessary, cut every five days and watered twice a night in summer. Any rogue seedlings of couch grass are weeded out by hand. And this entire *régime* of unrivalled cosseting contrasts spectacularly with a deliberately Spartan neglect of the trees, shrubs and flower borders. Here nothing is watered, not even the roses in summer. But they flourish nevertheless, because Scheinert has been careful to choose only plants that are adapted to hot, dry summers and therefore provide not only a stylish setting for the villa but also a link to the garrigue of the countryside that lies beyond La Casella.

Index

Acknowledgments

The publisher thanks the following photographers for their kind permission to reproduce the photographs in the book: Tim Beddow pp 54-9; Brian Chapple pp 172-7; Mick Hales pp 46-53, 192-7; Jerry Harpur pp 1-3, 6, 8-15, 24-37, 76-91, 104-31, 156-71, 178-91; Andrew Lawson pp 60-75, 98-103, 140-7; Vincent Motte pp 198-205; Walter Pfeiffer pp 4, 38-45; Charles Quest-Ritson pp 133-7, 139; Alex Ramsay pp 132, 138; Fritz von der Schulenberg pp 16-23; Jeremy Young 92-7, 148-55.

The publisher also thanks the following people and organizations for their kind permission to allow the use of their gardens in the book: Lord and Lady Carrington (pp8-15); John Stefanidis (pp16-23); The Marquess and Marchioness of Salisbury (pp24-31); Nicholas Haslam (pp33-7); Jim Reynolds (pp38-45); Marco Polo (pp46-53); Helen Dillon (pp54-9); Dr Ian Hamilton Finlay (pp60-67); The Gardeners Royal Benevolent Society (pp68-75); Capt and Mrs J Macdonald Buchanan (pp76-83); Christopher Lloyd (pp84-91); Winkworth Arboretum (pp92-7); Major and Mrs RA Colvile (pp98-103); Gordon Collier (pp104-9); Arabella Lennox-Boyd (pp110-17); Mr and Mrs Yeatman-Biggs (pp118-25); Mr George Gordon Macmillan of Macmillan (pp126-31); Signore Lauro Marchetti (pp132-9); John Hubbard (pp140-7); Pam Lewis (pp148-55); Jill Cowley (pp156-63); Lord and Lady Tollemache (pp164-71); Lord and Lady King (pp172-7); Mr and Mrs DH Cargill (pp178-83); Lord Lambton (pp184-91); Buzz Yudell and Tina Beebe (pp192-7); Tom Parr and Claus Scheinert (pp198-205).

Author's Acknowledgments

I would like to acknowledge the help and encouragement I have received from Tania Compton at House & Garden; Denise Bates, Clare Johnson, Emma Callery, Alison Shackleton and the team at Ebury Press; and above all, the owners and their staff, too numerous to list individually, for their invariable courtesy and helpfulness as I researched the gardens in this guide.